The Limits of Imagination

WORDSWORTH, YEATS, AND STEVENS

The Limits of Imagination

ꙅ WORDSWORTH, YEATS, and STEVENS

HELEN REGUEIRO

Cornell University Press   *Ithaca and London*

Cornell University Press gratefully acknowledges a grant
from the Andrew F. Mellon Foundation that aided
in bringing this book to publication.

Copyright © 1976 by Cornell University

First published 1976 by Cornell University Press.
Published in the United Kingdom by Cornell University Press Ltd.,
2–4 Brook Street, London W1Y 1AA.

Material from George Seferis, *Collected Poems 1924–1955,* translated
by Edmund Keeley and Philip Sherrard (copyright © 1967 by Princeton University Press; Princeton Paperback, 1975), pp. 15, 47, 95,
and 147–149, is reprinted by permission of Princeton University Press.

International Standard Book Number 0–8014–0994–2
Library of Congress Catalog Card Number 76–13663
Printed in the United States of America by York Composition Co., Inc.
*Librarians: Library of Congress cataloging information
appears on the last page of the book.*

For Samuel Elam

I am sorry for having let a broad river pass
    through my fingers
without drinking a single drop.

　　　　—George Seferis, "Mythistorema"

❧ CONTENTS

CONTENTS

≥ PREFACE

"Drink and be whole again beyond confusion." Frost's "Directive" addresses itself to what is perhaps the central concern of modern poetry—the quest for wholeness, the passage from isolation into being. Yet the bleakness of the landscape to which he returns and his need to "direct" us toward an unrealized state point to the incapacity of poetry to achieve its avowed ends. Poetry is the ritual, never the earth regained. And its mediational nature illuminates the dialectic it seeks constantly and unsuccessfully to transcend or to resolve. The dialectic has many names, but it is ultimately one between self and world, mind and nature, imagination and reality. Emerging from this dualism, poetry attempts to bridge the abyss that conditions its existence. It fails, of course, and its failure is the measure of its success. We may in fact see the history of poetry as the history of a mental traveler, punctuated by moments of vision and redemption.

These redemptive moments, as Geoffrey Hartman has pointed out, are associated with the imagination's capacity to transcend the self-consciousness that is the fall from being.[1] If self-consciousness is isolation and estrangement, imagination is the road to being, restoring the alienated self and reuniting the human with its spectre—fulfilling in this way the potential of man's humanity.

Much has been written in the last two decades on the necessity

1. "Romanticism and Anti-Self-Consciousness," *Beyond Formalism* (New Haven: Yale University Press, 1970).

for the imagination to triumph over self-consciousness and over reality, transcending the dialectic in which these two are engaged and redeeming the poetic self from its imprisonment in temporality. Yet the imagination, as the German romantics have shown us,[2] is itself intimately linked with self-consciousness, so that the movement of transcendence is paradoxically a movement inward that intensifies rather than resolves the dialectic, often leading to the ultimate estrangement: a solipsistic universe, or poetic silence, that is, poetic death. This book explores the dangers implicit in any unqualified affirmation of the imagination, since the forces that assail poetry lie not so much in reality as they do in the imagination itself. I have chosen three major poets whose work is grounded in the dialectical relationship of imagination and reality and whose imagination is engaged in a struggle with itself. Through them I have traced the poet's attempt to balance imagination and reality, his withdrawal and enclosure in self-consciousness, and his final return to a temporal and natural reality as the only realm where the imagination may continue to exist. The dialectic in the end affirms its own necessity rather than the necessity to resolve itself. Through the study of these poets I have tried to see modern poetry coming to recognize the dangers—and the limits—of imagination in its dealings with the exterior world, and accepting and affirming the tension that allows it to exist.

Wordsworth balances imagination and nature, resisting the thrust of inwardness, that is, of an autonomous imagination, even when its acknowledgment becomes inevitable. He searches for the wholeness of being in an alliance of mind and nature, though the mind may surreptitiously become "lord and master—outward sense / The obedient servant of her will" (*The Prelude*, XII, 222–223). The mind at times encompasses the natural world, but this encompassing is also a withdrawal. Wordsworth of course does not recognize the link between imagination and self-consciousness, yet the connection is made evident in moments of imaginative vision.

2. See again Hartman's "Romanticism and Anti-Self-Consciousness."

Yeats accepts the dialectical relationship of imagination and reality and opts, at least in his earlier poems, for the imaginatively constructed world. Self-consciousness thus becomes clearly associated with the imagination, and the dialectic moves into a different plane: no longer is it between imagination and nature, but between the imaginative act and the imaginative creation. The intensity of the act of creation seems to dispel a dialectic which, paradoxically, the finished creation brings more forcefully into focus. And the intentionally created world appears at the end removed from and invalidated by the natural reality it had initially denied. We witness in Yeats a curious movement back to the previous dialectic in order to contemplate a bleakness which the imagination will once again attempt to redeem. But Yeats understands, in a way that Wordsworth does not, the dangers of an imagination that wishes to become lord and master over reality and its own lord and master, achieving wholeness by containing the world as well as itself. The act of self-generation of course never takes place, and Yeats's recognition of the dangers of solipsism leads him to seek an imagination whose power and value derive precisely from its connection with the historical perspective.

Stevens' early poetry affirms the capacity of the imagination to transform a chaotic reality into a habitable place. Without imagination, the poet becomes the snowman, beholding "nothing that is not there and the nothing that is." The snowman is an indictment of human blindness, a description of a man without imagination, incapable of humanizing reality, of projecting himself into his world. Yet Stevens' "The Snow Man" holds a certain fascination, not only because it has two different meanings, but because through its two meanings we can trace the measure of Stevens' change in his attitude toward the imagination. More acutely than Yeats, Stevens comes to realize that the imagination transforms and destroys the real, leaving in its place painted strawberries and constructed pineapples. The dialectic, never ceasing to operate between imagination and reality, operates as well within the imagination, setting it against itself, against its own power to transform the given, so that imaginative transcendence no longer involves a transcendence of reality but a transcendence, as it were, of imagination itself. Stevens skirts silence almost to the extent that Hölderlin does, but he returns to poetic speech because he manages to build into the poem a recognition of its own limits, and through it a validation of the world the poet had initially sought to transform. "One walks easily / The unpainted shore, accepts the world / As anything but sculpture."[3] And so we return to the snowman. One *must,* indeed, "have a mind of winter," in order to perceive the wintry landscape without the trappings of self-consciousness, to perceive the landscape from within the landscape itself.[4] The more modern poetry recognizes the limits of imagination, the more the focus of the poem passes from the intentional act to a reality which paradoxically is made to exist by the poem itself. Poetry moves, simultaneously, in two apparently opposite directions: it recognizes, increasingly, the ability of the poetic act to "make reality," "a world of words to the end of it,"[5] and it posits, through the imagination's very dissatisfaction with itself, a world paradoxically "real," beyond the positings of the mind. The dialectic imagination-reality is at times transmuted into an inner dialectic, but never radically altered. Like Stevens at the end of his career, modern poetry attempts to return to "the plain sense of things" through the very language, the very self-consciousness that separate it from that world. Some things that go are gone, says the mountain to the belated traveler in search of spring in Ammons' "Eyesight." We are always one step away from, one moment past the spring. Poetry cannot reach that elusive moment by merely grasping, by merely saying. It can reach that moment only—if at all—by taking Hölderlin's "eccentric road" into itself, regenerating itself in its own failure and affirming the limits of the imaginative world.

3. Wallace Stevens, "So-And-So Reclining on Her Couch," in *The Collected Poems of Wallace Stevens* (New York: Knopf, 1954).

4. See Harold Bloom, *The Ringers in the Tower: Studies in Romantic Tradition* (Chicago: The University of Chicago Press, 1971), p. 281, and Hartman, *Beyond Formalism,* pp. 256–257.

5. Stevens, "Description without Place," VII, *Collected Poems.*

There is a trend in contemporary criticism to discard the categories of imagination and reality as valid critical terms and to view the relationships posited by the poem as existing within the poem itself. Thus Geoffrey Hartman sees Wordsworth in the Lucy poems removing "the mimetic dependence of imagination on reality."[6] Harold Bloom, too, sees the dialectical struggle no longer in terms of imagination and reality but of imagination and "imaginative priority."[7] And Paul de Man affirms the "literality" of the text by suggesting that the relationship in question is not one between subject and object but between subjects: "The relationship with nature has been superseded by an intersubjective, interpersonal relationship that, in the last analysis, is a relationship of the subject toward itself. Thus the priority has passed from the outside world entirely within the subject, and we end up with something that resembles a radical idealism."[8]

This view of reality at the level of poetic language bears certain affinities to a "new criticism" that reifies the literary text. The idea of a reified text is not new. As early as 1960, in his *Coleridge on Imagination*, I. A. Richards suggested that "the notion of reality derives from comparison between images, and to apply it as between images and things that are not images is an illegitimate extension which makes nonsense of it."[9]

Yet Bloom, de Man, and Hartman retain their dialectical criticism. Harold Bloom reads poetry in terms of a temporal dialectic between anteriority and belatedness (*The Anxiety of Influence*), or, as he puts it, a movement "from inside/outside polarities to early/late reversals."[10] Paul de Man, too, sees the image-object

6. *Beyond Formalism*, p. 50.
7. *The Anxiety of Influence: A Theory of Poetry* (New York: Oxford University Press, 1973), p. 72.
8. "The Rhetoric of Temporality," *Interpretation: Theory and Practice,* ed. Charles S. Singleton (Baltimore: The Johns Hopkins Press, 1969), p. 180.
9. Bloomington: Indiana University Press, p. 165.
10. *A Map of Misreading* (New York: Oxford University Press, 1975), p. 101. See also his *Kabbalah and Criticism* (New York: Seabury Press, 1975), p. 105.

polarity transformed into a temporal dialectic between an allegor-
ical sign and the "pure anteriority" of the previous sign.[11]
Geoffrey Hartman also reaffirms dialectical criticism through his
use of liminal categories and in his view of literature as "a highly
mediated art" that wishes "to dissolve as a medium or, at the
very least, to renounce romantic props and to intuit things
directly."[12]

Thus the focus of these critics' dialectical interpretations
shifts, from the categories of mind and nature to the world
which the imagination constructs and in which it moves, but
the essential tension remains—essential because this dialectical
approach unveils and preserves what is most valuable and most
significant about poetry, the struggle of each poem to create itself.
Poetry is not a smooth, sustained fiction of language. It is dark,
rugged, anxious, tragic, discontinuous, an act of the mind engaged in the creation of a threshold that may well destroy the
poem—and the poet who creates it.

What is particularly interesting about Richards' statement
quoted above is that, while it retains certain connections to the
criticism in which Bloom, de Man, and Hartman are engaged, it
seems to generate a type of interpretation diametrically opposed
to theirs, an interpretation that indeed reifies the literary text,
smooths out discontinuities, conceives of poetry as figuration.
Thus Joseph Riddel contends "that the act of poetry is a thing
itself, that 'things as they are' *are* only when contained in a mind,
or married to mind in a poem."[13] This kind of criticism seems at
first glance to be particularly suited to Stevens, since he claims
repeatedly that "it is a world of words to the end of it," that the
imagination is "the one reality / In this imagined world."[14] It

11. See "The Rhetoric of Temporality," pp. 190–191, and *Blindness
and Insight* (New York: Oxford University Press, 1971), p. 31.
12. See *Beyond Formalism,* pp. 349–350, and *The Fate of Reading*
(Chicago: The University of Chicago Press, 1971), p. 130; *Beyond Formalism,* p. ix.
13. *The Clairvoyant Eye: The Poetry and Poetics of Wallace Stevens*
(Baton Rouge: Louisiana State University Press, 1965), p. 144.
14. "Description without Place," VII, and "Another Weeping Woman,"
Collected Poems.

may indeed be argued that there are no poetic encounters of imagination and reality (logically there could not be), but encounters of images whose complex configurations constitute the experience of the poem. We may then argue that language is the only reality that poetry can lay claim to. This, too, is the case. Yet poetry struggles against the referential nature of the language that constitutes it, so that in effect it validates the dialectical approach which its apparent self-containment simultaneously brings into question. Perhaps in spite of themselves these poets argue for an imaginative world that exists within itself, and in which reality is itself figuration. Yeats and Stevens certainly go through that stage. Yet they return, at the end, to affirm a world outside the confines of their figurations, though paradoxically and inescapably through those figurations themselves. Metaphor is of course sustained, and poetry is sustained, but they are sustained by the very "degeneration" of that which permits them to exist. When Stevens speaks of "pure rhetoric," what he means is "a language without words."[15]

I have chosen to deal with Wordsworth, Yeats, and Stevens in terms of a criticism that retains the distinction between subject and object, self and world, imagination and reality, because these poets finally return to the snow they had forgotten, to the sound of the north wind.[16] They return, at least, to point to the inadequacies of their imaginative worlds, and a criticism that denies the existence of one of the terms of the dialectic cannot do justice to this "final finding of the ear."[17]

I wish to thank the Society for the Humanities, Cornell University, for a junior postdoctoral fellowship for the year 1973–1974, during which this book was conceived.

15. "Credences of Summer," IV, *Collected Poems.*
16. See Bloom, *The Ringers,* p. 281, and Roy Harvey Pearce, "The Last Lesson of the Master," *The Act of the Mind: Essays on the Poetry of Wallace Stevens,* ed. Roy Harvey Pearce and J. Hillis Miller (Baltimore: The Johns Hopkins Press, 1965), pp. 131, 141.
17. Stevens, "The Course of a Particular," *Collected Poems.*

Grateful acknowledgment is extended to the following:

Cornell University Press for material reprinted from A. R. Ammons, "Reflective," *Northfield Poems,* copyright © 1966 by Cornell University; and "Unsaid," *Selected Poems,* copyright © 1968 by Cornell University, used by permission of Cornell University Press.

Alfred A. Knopf, Inc., for material reprinted from Wallace Stevens, *The Collected Poems of Wallace Stevens,* copyright 1923, 1931, 1935, 1936, 1937, 1942, 1943, 1944, 1945, 1946, 1947, 1948, 1949, 1950, 1951, 1952, 1954 by Wallace Stevens; *The Necessary Angel,* copyright 1942, 1944, 1947, 1948, 1949, 1951 by Wallace Stevens; and *Opus Posthumous,* ed. Samuel French Morse, copyright 1957 by Elsie Stevens and Holly Stevens.

The Macmillan Publishing Company, Inc., for permission to reprint material from *The Collected Poems of W. B. Yeats:* "The Song of the Happy Shepherd" and "The Two Trees" (copyright 1906 by Macmillan Publishing Co., Inc., renewed 1934 by William Butler Yeats); "Ego Dominus Tuus" (copyright 1918 by Macmillan Publishing Co., Inc., renewed 1946 by Bertha Georgie Yeats); "The Wild Swans at Coole" and "The Living Beauty" (copyright 1919 by Macmillan Publishing Co., Inc., renewed 1947 by Bertha Georgie Yeats); "Towards Break of Day," "A Prayer for My Daughter," "Solomon and the Witch" (copyright 1924 by Macmillan Publishing Co., Inc., renewed 1952 by Bertha Georgie Yeats); "Nineteen Hundred and Nineteen" and "Sailing to Byzantium" (copyright 1928 by Macmillan Publishing Co., Inc., renewed 1956 by Georgie Yeats); "Tom the Lunatic," "A Dialogue of Self and Soul," "Byzantium" (copyright 1933 by Macmillan Publishing Co., Inc., renewed 1961 by Bertha Georgie Yeats); "A Crazed Girl" and "Lapis Lazuli" (copyright 1940 by Georgie Yeats, renewed 1968 by Bertha Georgie Yeats, Michael Butler Yeats, and Anne Yeats) and for material reprinted from *A Vision* by W. B. Yeats (copyright 1937 by William Butler Yeats, renewed 1965 by Bertha Georgie Yeats and Anne Butler Yeats).

Faber and Faber Ltd for material from Wallace Stevens, *The*

Collected Poems of Wallace Stevens, The Necessary Angel, and *Opus Posthumous;* reprinted by permission of Faber and Faber Ltd.

Jonathan Cape Ltd for permission to reprint material from George Seferis, *Collected Poems 1924–1955,* trans., ed., and introd. by Edmund Keeley and Philip Sherrard.

Oxford University Press for permission to reprint material from *The Poetical Works of William Wordsworth,* ed. by E. de Selincourt and Helen Darbishire; and from *The Prelude* by William Wordsworth, ed. Ernest de Selincourt, 2d ed. revised by Helen Darbishire.

A. P. Watt & Son for material reprinted from *The Collected Poems of W. B. Yeats* and from *A Vision* by W. B. Yeats, by permission of M. B. Yeats, Miss Anne Yeats, and The Macmillan Company of London & Basingstoke.

HELEN REGUEIRO

New Haven, Connecticut

ᴺ NOTE ON THE TEXTS

The following texts and abbreviations are used:

The Poetical Works of William Wordsworth, edited from the manuscripts with textual and critical notes by E. de Selincourt and Helen Darbishire. 5 vols. Oxford: The Clarendon Press, 1940–1949.

William Wordsworth, *The Prelude,* edited from the manuscripts with introduction, textual and critical notes by Ernest de Selincourt. 2d ed., revised by Helen Darbishire. Oxford: The Clarendon Press, 1959.

The Collected Poems of W. B. Yeats. New York: The Macmillan Company, 1956. (*CP*)

The Collected Poems of Wallace Stevens. New York: Alfred A. Knopf, 1954. (*CP*)

Wallace Stevens, *Opus Posthumous,* edited, with an introduction, by Samuel French Morse. New York: Alfred A. Knopf, 1957. (*OP*)

The Limits of Imagination

WORDSWORTH, YEATS, AND STEVENS

⚹ INTRODUCTION

I found a
weed
that had a

mirror in it
and that
mirror

looked in at
a mirror
in

me that
had a
weed in it   [A. R. Ammons, "Reflective"]

Ammons' poem establishes an identity between the self and the
natural object. The natural world mirrors the self, but the self is
itself in the process of mirroring the natural world. Container and
contained are indistinguishable, and this identity in turn abolishes
the distinction between subject and object, between the act of
participation and the act of possession. Self and weed are both
perceivers and perceived, and the act of perception of each involves both the perception of the exterior object and of the self.
In other words, the self and the world contain and reflect each
other. Reflection points not to alienation, but to an infinite potential for identity.

The weed reflecting the self that reflects the weed establishes also an identity between inwardness and exteriority. The act of imaginative perception is a pathway into the natural world. Rather, the identity between subject and object precludes any distinction between imagination and reality. What is interesting about this poem is Ammons' refusal to grant the poetic imagination any greater importance or validity than that which he grants to the natural world. The balance between the poetic imagination and the natural object is so perfectly maintained that the tension between them dissolves, and becomes integration.[1]

Yet the necessity to establish such balance, to affirm such identity, points to the dialectical relationship between imagination and reality that informs Western poetry. The imagination arises when the unity of self and world has been lost, and its paradoxical function is to retrieve the unity whose loss gave it birth—to enter, through consciousness, a world from which all consciousness is excluded. Hopkins quite accurately terms the imagination "the widow of an insight lost."[2] For it exists only as absence, only as a hope that feeds on its own failure. In *The Temptation of the West* Malraux uses the Oedipus myth to illuminate this peculiar relationship of imagination and reality in the Western world and interprets the legend in terms of the Cartesian dialectic. "The Western world is born there, with the hard face of Minerva. . . . After the death of the Sphinx, Oedipus turns in upon himself."[3] By pitting his intelligence against the outside world, symbolized here by the Sphinx, Oedipus destroys the world he might have inhabited. Yet the very conception of the legend points to the outside world as a place of danger. Oedipus has to choose not between affirming the

1. This statement itself breaks down the balance which I am arguing Ammons' poem achieves, since balance is established by an assertion of the poetic imagination itself.

2. "To R. B."

3. André Malraux, *La Tentation de l'Occident* (Paris: Grasset, 1926). "L'Occident naît là, avec le dur visage de Minerve. . . . Après la mort du Sphinx, Oedipe s'attaque à lui-même" (pp. 68–69). All translations, unless otherwise noted, are my own.

self and affirming the being-in-the-world, but between affirming
the self and being destroyed by reality. Inwardness and exteriority
are already at odds. Only the Chinese, Malraux goes on, can
"imagine . . . without images," so that "the idea of the world,
of the world which he could not imagine, corresponds for him to
a reality."[4] Imagination and reality, the poetic image and the
natural object, appear in the West opposed and inimical to each
other's existence. To re-enter reality the imagination must annihilate itself. To continue to sing, it must retain its distance and
affirm the dialectic. It is this instinctive recognition of the mutual
exclusiveness of imagination and reality that makes Rilke's
Orpheus, in the twenty-third sonnet, intentionally turn and lose
Eurydice a second time. To regain her is to abandon himself to
the plentitude of things. In choosing to "perceive" her he chooses
to perceive her in her absence, to constantly attempt her reappearance through his song.[5]

Eurydice's "reappearance," of course, never takes place. When
Borges defines the aesthetic phenomenon as "this imminence of
a revelation which does not occur,"[6] he too is pointing to the
mutual exclusiveness of the ontologically valid experience and its
aesthetic representation. To attempt a resolution of this dialectic
is either to create a world "in nature's spite"[7] or to risk drowning
in the plentitude of things. The initial and essential opposition between consciousness and reality out of which poetry emerges
seems to make most poets feel that a "resolution," if such there be,

---

4. The passage in its entirety is as follows: "Le Chinois imagine, si je
puis dire, sans images. C'est cela qui le fait s'attacher à la qualité et non
au personnage, à la sagesse et non à l'empéreur. C'est pour cela que l'idée
du monde, du monde qu'il ne saurait imaginer, correspond pour lui à une
réalité" (p. 108).

5. "Aber immer wieder weggedreht, / wenn du meinst, sie endlich zu
erfassen" ("But always again turning away, / when you feel you are finally
grasping it"), Sonnets to Orpheus, II, 23. See Maurice Blanchot, L'Espace
littéraire (Paris: Gallimard, 1955), "Le regard d'Orphée," esp. p. 232.

6. Jorge Luis Borges, "The Wall and the Books," Labyrinths (New
York: New Directions, 1962), p. 188.

7. W. B. Yeats, "Coole Park, 1929."

lies in either extreme, not in a balance that would compromise the integrity of each. Yet these are extremes whose attainment is most often purchased by the loss of power, and invariably at great personal cost. To re-create and contain the world, or to become one with reality, is to reduce to silence the poetic voice that exists to name the absence of things. Hölderlin's "der Gesang . . . glückt" (the song succeeds)[8] foreshadows the "Tinian" fragment in which he discovers that golden and thoughtlike blossoms, "sprung from themselves," are dangerous to pick:

> Die Blumen giebt es,
> Nicht von der Erde gezeugt, von selber
> Aus lokerem Boden sprossen die,
> Ein Widerstral des Tages, nicht ist
> Es ziemend, diese zu pflüken,
> Denn golden stehen,
> Unzubereitet,
> Ja schon die unbelaubten
> Gedanken gleich.

> There are flowers
> Not sprung from the earth, from themselves
> Out of the empty soil they spring,
> A reflection of day, and it is not
> Proper to pick these,
> For they stand golden,
> Unprepared,
> Leafless
> Like thoughts.

Flowers sprung not from the earth, but from the empty soil of consciousness, point once again to the rift that exists between the poet's inner world and the universe of things.

The pervasiveness of this barren landscape is the starting point and very often the end result of the poetic act. "Where man is not, nature is barren," Blake tells us. But Blake is perhaps unique in discarding the dialectical relationship between imagination and nature. Nature is the road to Ulro, and the question the imagina-

---

8. "Wie wenn am Feiertage."

tion must raise with regard to nature is the poet's question to Tirzah: "What have I to do with thee?"[9] Blake's world is thus less vulnerable—if vulnerable at all—to the opposition between consciousness and reality, imagination and nature. With one of the poles of the dialectic rendered invalid, the poet can affirm the ontological necessity of Jerusalem, the flaming city created by the poetic act. Yet for most poets it is precisely *because* man is there that nature is barren. The imagination seldom if ever has such unqualified validity. Stevens' jar may order the slovenly wilderness around it, but it is also incapable of giving "of bird or bush." And the man with the blue guitar recognizes that he "cannot bring a world quite round" though he may "patch it as [he] can." Distanced from the natural world by the consciousness that brings poetry into being, the poet is equally distanced from it by the poetry that constructs an intentional landscape. "We live in a place / That is not our own and, much more, not ourselves," Stevens goes on.[10] Yet to make the world both "our own" and "ourselves" the poet has to construct, intentionally, a world that includes the natural.[11] Though the imaginative act is an attempt to bridge the abyss between consciousness and reality, whether it seeks an immediate experience of the object or the containment of reality the poetic imagination creates an enclosed space that mirrors and rejects the poet's endless attempts to create a place of being. And the dialectic remains unresolved. The problem faced by poets in the nineteenth and twentieth centuries is that they must affirm the act of consciousness that isolates them from the world they wish to enter, and this affirmation forces upon them the barren landscape which they repeatedly fail to sacralize. Yeats speaks of "the desolation of reality."[12] For

9. William Blake, "Proverbs of Hell," *The Marriage of Heaven and Hell,* and "To Tirzah," *Songs of Experience.*

10. "Notes toward a Supreme Fiction" ("It Must Be Abstract," IV).

11. For a discussion of the poetic image and the dialectic between the natural and the intentional, see Paul de Man, "Intentional Structure of the Romantic Image," *Romanticism and Consciousness: Essays in Criticism,* ed. Harold Bloom (New York: Norton, 1970), pp. 65–77.

12. "Supernatural Songs," XII.

Hölderlin "silent is the Delphic god, and long the paths have lain solitary and waste."[13] Rimbaud encounters "les déserts de l'amour." And Seferis perceives reality as an endless sea, on which the voyagers travel with broken oars.[14] The initial distinction between subject and object pervades Western art and makes the attempted resolution a further intensification of the dialectic. When Richard III says "I am myself alone" he is speaking to us with a peculiarly modern voice. The affirmation of self is invariably followed by the experience of isolation.[15] The subject conscious of his subjectivity looks upon the objective world as an alien place, a place which he can neither re-create nor inhabit.

Emerson's complaint in "Nature" that "the axis of vision is not coincident with the axis of things, and so they appear not transparent but opaque" is the metaphorical equivalent of Shakespeare's recognition of the Cartesian dialectic. Coleridge, too, in "Dejection: An Ode" speaks of a blank eye, a complaint foreshadowed by his statement a year earlier in a letter to Godwin that "the Poet is dead in [him]." The ability to perceive reality "immaculately"[16] is directly linked to the poet's ability to write poetry. Though Wordsworth will later affirm the necessity to distance himself from nature in order to become a "creative soul," both he and Coleridge develop theories of the imagination whose thrust it is to contain and resolve the loss of the child's immediate perception of things. When Coleridge tells us that the "primary imagination" is "a repetition in the finite mind of the eternal act of creation in the infinite I AM,"[17] he is asserting an underlying oneness between the human and the natural and, more important for Wordsworth, between the natural and the transcendent. The

13. "Stumm ist der delphische Gott, und einsam liegen und öde / Längst die Pfade," "Der Archipelagus."

14. "Mythistorema," 12, Collected Poems 1924–1955, trans., ed., and introd. by Edmund Keeley and Philip Sherrard (Princeton: Princeton University Press), 1967.

15. See Northrop Frye, Fools of Time (Toronto, University of Toronto Press, 1967), chap. 3: "Little World of Man: The Tragedy of Isolation."

16. See Friedrich Nietzsche, Also Sprach Zarathusthra, chap. 37.

17. Biographia Literaria, XIII.

movement of ascension that we witness in Wordsworth points, in fact, to this attempt to connect two disparate perspectives. The vision of the imagination achieved in the Alps binds the natural and the transcendent and allows the poet to affirm the force that "rolls through all things." Yet the vision of the imagination is not unselfconscious. Not only does it emerge "unfathered" and from the mind's abyss,[18] but the movement upward is paralleled by a movement inward, by a growing rift between inwardness and exteriority, between the human self and the natural world.

Yet Wordsworth maintains the unselfconscious nature of the imagination, and it is because he rejects the notion of self-consciousness in reference to the imaginative process that he is able to come down, twice, from the Alps. He returns telling us that what he has seen is a vision that binds and contains, one which the poet can participate in, but which he cannot possess. The dimension of transcendence is thus sustained. Wordsworth is more successful than most poets in maintaining this balance between inwardness and exteriority, the natural and the transcendent. He is content to leave as they are "the untransmuted shapes of many worlds."[19] But Shelley, also in a movement of ascension, sculpts the "unsculptured image" of the summits and discovers that he has sculpted his own image. "Mont Blanc," indeed, makes clear the path that the imagination embarks on, rejecting the experiential richness of the natural for the absolute reality of the summits only to discover, at the end, that it was a conception of the absolute generated by the self. It is precisely when the poet discovers that the exterior world is actually created by his act of perception that the poetic enterprise, whose goal it was to arrive at this absolute "Power," fails. To discover oneself creator of the world is to discover that there is no world one can inhabit.

18. See Harold Bloom, *The Visionary Company: A Reading of English Romantic Poetry* (New York: Doubleday, 1961), p. 148, and Geoffrey H. Hartman, *The Unmediated Vision: An Interpretation of Wordsworth, Hopkins, Rilke, and Valéry* (New York: Harcourt, Brace & World, 1966), p. 13.
19. *The Prelude*, VI, 464.

> Of its own beauty is the mind diseased,
> And fevers into false creation:—where,
> Where are the forms the sculptor's soul hath seiz'd?
> In him alone.[20]

This recognition that one is the creator of one's world is coupled with the inability to accept such a world. The poet is simultaneously denied access to the world he has created, and trapped within its confines. Wordsworth contends that the poet is "creator and receiver both," that he works "in alliance" with nature. At the end of "Mont Blanc," on the other hand, the Shelleyan imagination has transformed the profusion of the natural into a wasteland of ice. The elemental continuity of ice and river is broken by the prospect of destruction. There is no descent once the poet has recognized the "Power [that] dwells apart in its tranquillity" as existing within himself. Shelley arrives at the conclusion that Wordsworth so carefully avoids in the ascension passages of *The Prelude*. Though Wordsworth's vapor is "unfathered," the mind is "lost" and contained within a force larger than itself. In Shelley's poem the Power that dwells "remote, serene, and inaccessible" is recognized to be the imagination itself. Coleridge's distinction between the primary and the secondary imagination breaks down in "Mont Blanc," and the primary imagination passes into the conscious, intentional act of perception-creation of the poet's mind:

> And what were thou, and earth, and stars, and sea,
> If to the human mind's imaginings
> Silence and solitude were vacancy?

Wordsworth's sudden halt leads him into a moment of illumination, a vision of the transcendent. Shelley is forced, at the end, to gaze on "this, the naked countenance of earth." Barrenness and desolation are at the beginning of the poetic act and also, often, at its close.

Yeats seeks to escape this desolation of reality by constructing a fully intentional and self-contained world. But he finds, in the

20. Lord Byron, *Childe Harold's Pilgrimage,* Canto IV, CXXII.

intemporal world of Byzantium, that the poetic self is reduced
and silenced by its "resolution" of the dialectic, by its very imperviousness to nature and to time. When inwardness successfully
contains and annihilates exteriority, poet and protagonist become
distinct. The fictional self within the poem, in "Sailing to
Byzantium," is silenced by the very absolute which it sought, and
the poet, remaining within the temporal perspective and distinguishing himself from his protagonist, writes a poem about the
death of the creative self. Such distinctions between poet and
protagonist are not uncommon in nineteenth- and twentieth-
century poetry. And they point, invariably, to an intensification
of the dialectic which they wish to synthesize. Coleridge writes a
poem about his protagonist's ability to both create and inhabit
the pleasure dome. But he remains, the introduction to the poem
notwithstanding,[21] outside the confines of Kubla Khan's world.
Stevens too discovers that not only is the intentionally created
world "gray and bare," but it is one which he cannot enter and
still remain a poet. The gate into Byzantium is "the gate / To the
enclosure."[22] The poet is often faced with a choice between entering the intentional world and becoming, like Yeats's protagonist, a
mechanical golden bird that can sing "of what is past, or passing,
or to come," which means not sing at all, or rejecting the intentional creation and remaining within the tension of the unresolved
dialectic ("Good-bye, / Mrs. Pappadopoulos, and thanks"[23]).

Stevens is particularly aware of the problems associated with
the intentional. He knows that language falsifies ("In the way
you speak / You arrange, the thing is posed, / What in nature
merely grows"[24]), that "metaphor [is] degeneration," and that
the world of the singer in "The Idea of Order at Key West" must

21. " . . . if that indeed be called composition in which all the images
rose up before him as things, with a parallel production of the correspondent expressions, without any sensation or consciousness of effort." He
goes on to say, though, that once interrupted all the rest passes away
"like the images on the surface of a stream into which a stone has been
cast, but, alas! without the after restoration of the latter!"
22. Stevens, "The Rock," III.
23. Stevens, "So-And-So Reclining on Her Couch."
24. "Add This to Rhetoric."

be protected from the assault of the poetic imagination. There is a core of silence in his poems, an avowal of the incapacity of poetry to name or create the world it seeks. Yet it is this recognition of the dangers inherent in poetic speech that allows the song of the protagonist to be conceived within the poem but placed beyond the verbal construct. The subject of the poem becomes in fact the inability of the poem to become song, to transcend the intentional creation and become an immediate expression of the oneness of self and world. The girl's song in the poem orders and masters the poet's vision of reality. But within the poem itself the poet witnesses the song's end. When Hölderlin says "bald sind [wir] aber Gesang" (soon we will be song),[25] he expects poetry to resacralize reality, to bring the multiple gods back into existence. But when the poem succeeds in this way, it equally silences itself in the reality of things. Poetry seems to walk a narrow ridge between the quest for the absolute, which involves an abstractive imagination that in its ascension distances itself from the natural world, and the quest for immediacy, which requires what Stevens calls "a letting down / From loftiness,"[26] a rejection of the transcendent and a redescent into the natural world. At either extreme lie silence and death. The success of the intentional construct spells at best a clear distinction between poet and protagonist, at worst an enclosure in an imaginative world that to be complete must reject its relation to the natural. The success of the poem's desire to reach the immediacy of the object results either in the recognition of its impossibility, or in the poem's drowning in reality. Stevens shows us in "Metaphors of a Magnifico" the process of the poem breaking down and becoming the unsung song of the fruit trees. And Hölderlin in "Hälfte des Lebens" foreshadows the silence of his madness in the image of the trees, overladen with fruit, bending down toward their image in the lake. Once Narcissus sees his image in the water he loses his capacity to see the water. A zone of consciousness is forever interposed be-

25. "Friedensfeier."
26. "The Sail of Ulysses," V.

tween him and the natural world. To become one with his image
and regain the wholeness he has lost, he must drown into reality,
abandoning his ability to perceive it. The poet becomes one with
the song at the price of poetry itself.

It is for this reason that Hölderlin terms poetry "der Güter
Gefährlichstes," the most dangerous of possessions.[27] When the
weathercocks silently crow,[28] when the intentional has become one
with the natural, the poet faces the imminence of silence, of poetic
death. The silent crow of the weathercocks signals either the
recognition that language is unable to "dichten" ("poematize"[29])
reality, or the final consummation in which language becomes
experience, the image coincides with the object, and poetry
drowns in the reality of things. Similarly Keats in "Ode to a
Nightingale" is faced with the choice of following the bird—
becoming one with the natural—or retaining his otherness to
create a poem about immediacy and loss. Yeats too understands
the danger of being "struck dumb in the simplicity of fire."[30]
Poetry inevitably is an act by which the poet is tolled back to his
sole self, a self which he rarely though occasionally abandons,
but one whose isolation he must sustain in order for the muse to
sing. In a sense, this is what happens with Wordsworth's encounters. He remains solidly within the temporal perspective,
absorbing the moment of vision into the natural but refusing to
allow himself to dissolve. To dissolve is to die poetically, and the
growth of the poet's mind depends precisely on the poet's ability
to account for distance and loss in terms of evolution. Thus when
he encounters the solitary reaper he listens without entering or
attempting to enter the world of the song—not because poetic
entrance means destruction, as it does for Stevens, but because the
meaning of the encounter is to be found in the temporal world

27. "Aber in Hütten wohnet der Mensch," *Bruchstücke und Entwürfe*.
28. "In lieblicher Bläue."
29. There is no appropriate translation of "dichten." It means "to
make" a poem in the way an artisan makes a chair.
30. "Vacillation," VII.

rather than in the natural perspective in which it takes place. The dialectic between the natural and the intentional, which operates so clearly in Stevens, and less clearly in Yeats, becomes at times in Wordsworth a dialectic between the natural and the temporal, one in which the poet is confronted by an infinitely valuable world from which he must "gently pass." To remain would be to abandon the poetic enterprise, to find himself not in the place of the poet looking mutely down at the grave of the boy of Winander, but in the grave itself, at one with natural things.

This disjunction between the natural and the intentional is for the most part inescapable and also essential to poetic creation. In "Mr. Stratis Thalassinos Describes a Man," Seferis speaks of an infinitesimal grain of sand that stands between the poet and the ultimate self-surrender:

But there's still something: an infinitesimal obstacle, a grain of sand, shrinking and shrinking yet unable to disappear completely. I don't know what I ought to say or what I ought to do. Sometimes that obstacle seems to me like a teardrop wedged into some articulation of the orchestra, keeping it silent until it's been dissolved. And I have an unbearable feeling that all the rest of my life won't be sufficient to dissolve this drop within my soul. And I'm haunted by the thought that, if they were to burn me alive, this obstinate moment would be the last to surrender.[31]

It is not difficult to guess that the infinitesimal and persistent grain of sand is an image of consciousness, a consciousness which can destroy and annihilate the world and still not transcend or eradicate itself. Consciousness is that "slightest distance"[32] between the poet and reality which allows him—indeed impels him—to create. To achieve the right angle of vision, the right approach into the object, the right proximity beyond which object and poem disappear—this is one of the major concerns of modern poetry. If poetic language is the most dangerous of possessions, this is because it may try to capture the object, grip it "in savage

31. *Collected Poems*, pp. 147–149.
32. "Mythistorema," 8, *Collected Poems*, p. 23.

scrutiny,"[33] and capture only the object's absence, or it may be too successful indeed, and silence itself in its recovery of being. Also in "Mr. Stratis Thalassinos Describes a Man," Seferis speaks of a flame that goes out if the balance within which it exists is altered:

What can a flame remember? If it remembers a little less than is necessary, it goes out; if it remembers a little more than is necessary, it goes out. If only it could teach us, while it burns, to remember correctly.[34]

Though poetry is almost invariably a search for extreme resolutions, only within this balance, which entails a recognition of its limitations, can it sustain itself. This is, perhaps, the meaning of remembering correctly: recognizing the limits of imagination, that the act of trespassing may not forever wed Orpheus to Eurydice, or construct an intentional world in nature's spite.

It is such a world that Baudelaire wishes to construct in "Paysage" (*Les Fleurs du mal*, LXXXVI). He attempts to transmute the intentional into the natural, to create a season in an inner world:

> Et quand viendra l'hiver aux neiges monotones,
> Je fermerai partout portières et volets
> Pour bâtir dans la nuit mes féeriques palais.
> Alors je rêverai des horizons bleuâtres,
> Des jardins, des jets d'eau pleurant dans les albâtres,
> Des baisers, des oiseaux chantant soir et matin,
> Et tout ce que l'Idylle a de plus enfantin.
> L'Emeute, tempêtant vainement à ma vitre,
> Ne fera pas lever mon front de mon pupitre;
> Car je serai plongé dans cette volupté
> D'évoquer le Printemps avec ma volonté,
> De tirer un soleil de mon cœur, et de faire
> De mes pensers brûlants une tiède atmosphère.

> And when winter comes with its monotonous snows
> I shall everywhere close curtains and shutters
> To erect in the night my magical palaces.

33. Stevens, "Credences of Summer," VII.
34. *Collected Poems*, p. 147.

> I shall then dream of blue horizons,
> Of gardens, of fountains weeping on alabaster,
> Of kisses, of birds singing evening and morning,
> Of everything most childish and idyllic.
> The Tumult vainly storming at my window
> Will not make my head lift from my desk;
> For I shall be immersed in the voluptuousness
> Of evoking the Spring with my will,
> Of drawing a sun from my heart, and of making
> Of my burning thoughts a warm atmosphere.

To create, intentionally, a natural world, the poet must close off his inner world—"I shall everywhere close curtains and shutters" —but the enclosure itself points to the failure of his attempt. Like Yeats's "Sailing to Byzantium," with the protagonist impervious to the changes of the temporal or the natural, Baudelaire's protagonist is unmoved by the raging storm outside. But the poetic act does not suffice, and ultimately Baudelaire undertakes the final voyage, "au fond de l'Inconnu pour trouver du nouveau" (to the bottom of the Unknown to find the new).[35]

Seferis, on the other hand, posits a world "beyond the broken statues," one which the poetic act can neither reach nor help him to forget, and a storm which he chooses not to disregard:

> The garden with its fountains in the rain:
> you will see it only from the low window
> behind clouded glass. Your room
> will be lit only by the flames from the fireplace
> and sometimes the distant lightning will reveal
> the wrinkles on your forehead, my old Friend.

> The garden with the fountains that in your hands
> was a rhythm of the other life beyond the broken
> statues and the tragic columns
> and a dance among the oleanders
> beside the new quarries,
> misty glass will have cut off from your days.
> You won't breathe; earth and the sap of the trees

35. "Le Voyage," *Les Fleurs du mal*, CXXVI.

> will spring from your memory to strike
> this window struck by the rain
> from the outside world.   ["Mythistorema," 6][36]

Seferis evokes in this poem the garden of childhood, a world in which reality merged with reality and in which the relationship of self and world had the fluidity of water meeting water—the "fountains in the rain." But the garden is part of the past, and the poet recollects it behind clouded glass, cut off from this realm of oneness by a zone of consciousness that, like the grain of sand, nothing can dissolve. The clouded glass also suggests, beyond the opacity of consciousness (one is reminded of Emerson's notion of opacity when "the axis of vision is not coincident with the axis of things"), a perception of natural reality blurred by the temporal perspective. But there is, in Seferis' poem, a remnant of reality, a distant lightning that reminds the poet of a natural world beyond his enclosed space and reveals at the same time, with his wrinkled forehead, the ravages of time.

The garden, too, suggests more than the child's first world. It points to the ancient world of Greece, where art was not art but *techne,* artisanship, and where the imaginative act was an act not of consciousness but of reality itself. The rhythm of the other life intimates this oneness of the self with natural reality from which the poet remains separated by the opacity of misty, clouded glass.

The last four lines suggest a possibility of passage between these two worlds. The natural world has remained hauntingly present outside the enclosed world of the poem, barely visible through the misty glass, but unquestionably there. It rises now to strike against the window of consciousness, and in a parallel movement the poet's remembrance of a more immediate reality springs from this side of consciousness to pass into the reality outside the conscious self. Remembrance and rain fight the divisiveness of consciousness and attempt to transform the space of alienation between them into the essential garden and the other life. The window, which

36. *Collected Poems,* p. 15.

blocks vision, can also make vision possible. Poetry can transform
opacity into transparence, remembrance into restoration.

This dual force of memory and rain, the force of the inner and
outer worlds seeking to reunite the fragmented self, is beautifully
captured in the verb *ktypo,* which means to strike, to hit, as well
as to call, to knock, to ring—a destructive force, but also a wish
to gain admittance into an unimaginable world. It is as if the
memory of immediacy and the natural force from the outside
were forces seeking to destroy the clouded glass and also symbolic
knockings on the door of consciousness, seeking passage between
two alien worlds. Consciousness is thus conceived not only as a
barrier between the self and the world, but also as a possible passage between them—a window that might be broken or cleared,
a door that might be, as in Dickinson's world, left ajar.

This distance that is equally distance and proximity suggests
an opening up of the poem, a recognition of the limits of poetry
which paradoxically makes possible an unmediated experience.
Baudelaire refuses to be diverted by the storm outside and reaffirms his isolation. Seferis, like Yeats and Stevens, grounds the
poem in a recognition of its intentionality, and makes it thus a
rite of passage into a world avowedly beyond its reach.

Wordsworth is not as concerned as Yeats or Stevens with the
intentional quality of poetic creation. Poetry is not just an act of
the mind, but both the cause and the result of an alliance between
the human and the natural. The dialectic operates for him between the temporal and the natural, and between the natural and
the transcendent. We have in his poems about childhood two distinct worlds defined in terms of the inhabitant's perception of temporality. The poet watches the child refute the notion of death
("We Are Seven"), affirming the spatial as well as metaphysical
continuity between grass and grave. He watches the dead Lucy become part of the natural world. At the same time, the desire to
pass into the natural perspective is overwhelmed by a desire to
contain and resolve the existing tension and the feeling of loss.
Wordsworth's poetry is not a poetry of extremes, but one in which
the balance is always kept by a meditation on the gain rather than

the loss. Nature becomes less ontologically important, and the vision of the transcendent, whose parallel inwardness Wordsworth refuses to acknowledge, becomes the central experience in the later works. It is, paradoxically, a vision of the absolute sustained within the temporal perspective, a transcendence of temporality achieved by an affirmation of time against the intrusion of the natural. Eliot tells us in *Four Quartets* that "human kind / Cannot bear very much reality" (referring to the isolated moment of immediacy), and that time "protects mankind from heaven and damnation / Which flesh cannot endure."[37] Wordsworth systematically places the moment of experience within the context of duration, and the experience derives its value from the remembrance it provides. Memory, in fact, seems less a function of time than of eternity. It places the poet in a privileged position in which poetry is of necessity more balanced and also by definition less assaulted by the dangers of nature or self-consciousness. Wordsworth seems simultaneously to yearn for a vision of nature irretrievably lost and to reject the "powerless trance" in which nature has held him— simultaneously to affirm the validity of the transcendent and to grieve for the loss of the particular. That the tension remains despite his protestations bears witness to the complexity which Wordsworth himself overlooks.

Yeats bypasses entirely Wordsworth's distinction between the temporal and the natural. The natural *is* the temporal, a world of process, of history, in which the self is assailed and finally destroyed. Yeats begins by withdrawing from the historical process, by creating an intentional world, an "artifice of eternity" in which the self can be totally itself and its world. Where Wordsworth seeks transcendence from the natural by affirming an imaginative vision which he cannot fully capture, Yeats affirms the intentional quality of poetic creation. The rival of the created world, he looks for the face he had "before the world was made."[38] He seeks to create both himself and his world, to transcend the historical perspective

37. "Burnt Norton," I, II.
38. "Before the World Was Made."

in which his desire for order is constantly undercut by the meaninglessness of events. Thus Yeats creates a world in nature's spite,
but one in which the poet must distinguish himself from his protagonist, and in which he witnesses the death of the protagonist's
creativity. The achieved resolution becomes inimical to poetic
creation. The transcendence of the natural and the historical
forces the protagonist to fall into the silence of simple things.
Complexity, in fact, seems to be the generating principle of Yeats's
poetry. In the second of the "Byzantium" poems the poet recognizes the danger which the protagonist succumbed to in the first,
and instead of reducing intricacy to simplicity he has the smithies
of the emperor "break bitter furies of complexity," in the dual
sense, as Bloom points out, of "mar" and "create."[39] Though historical complexity leaves the self unsatisfied, the achieved simplicity leaves it silent and in that sense dead. Coleridge's "the Poet is
dead in me"[40] applies in modern poetry to the achieved resolution
rather than to the sustaining of the dialectic.[41] Yeats finally moves
from the intentional back to the historical, rejecting the intemporality of art for the process which poetry constantly redeems.

Stevens begins with a sense of the meaninglessness of the natural unless informed by the imaginative. The poet must interpret
reality or be faced with "no-thingness." He must order and render
meaningful the wilderness world. Yet these poems of order, for
which Stevens is perhaps best known, are less a quest for the absolute than an attempt to give meaning to a more limited space.
The jar creates order in Tennessee, the oboe plays only asides, and
the poet writes only the notes toward a supreme fiction. The titles

39. Harold Bloom, *Yeats* (New York: Oxford University Press, 1970),
p. 392.
40. Letter to William Godwin, March 25, 1801.
41. See Paul de Man, "Tentation de la permanence," *Monde nouveau,*
10th year (Oct. 1955), pp. 49–61: "Far from being anti-historical, the
poetic act (in the general sense that includes all the arts) is pre-eminently
a historical act: one through which we become conscious of the divided
character of our being and, as a result, of the need to fulfill it, to create it
in time, rather than submit to it in eternity" (p. 53).

themselves suggest the limited scope of the poet's enterprise. This limitation, however, has a philosophical basis, stemming from the recognition of the dangers of the absolute which Wordsworth bypasses and which Yeats confronts and finally abandons. Yet even in these poems of order, Stevens recognizes the incapacity of the poetic word to approximate the "thingness" of the object. There are no "letters of rock and water,"[42] and the poetic image alienates rather than informs. Or rather the information is itself a betrayal of the natural object. Stevens feels more keenly than Wordsworth or Yeats the tension between the natural and the intentional, and his poetry is a slow process of separation of the creative from the rhetorical imagination. The temptation of the imagination is constantly to order and control, to create a world in which the poet may be himself and his world. From this "temptation of permanence,"[43] from the affirmation of the necessity of order and the recognition of imaginative enclosure, Stevens moves to an affirmation of the particular, an affirmation also of the limits of poetry when it attempts to establish contact with the natural world. The poem's recognition of its inability to reach the natural object forces upon it a meditation on itself, on the limits of its intentionality. It conceives of the natural world and simultaneously places that world beyond its reach. Paradoxically, this poetry of decreation, which utters only its inability to reach the natural object and which approaches the object only as absence, makes possible within the poem the unmediated experience of the world it cannot reach. The clouded glass of Seferis' poem, assailed by the inner and outer worlds, finds its counterpart in the bronze decor of Stevens' palm "at the end of the mind,"[44] where the space of alienation is transformed into the threshold of being. The natural and the intentional, at odds from the beginning, are synthesized, for a moment, when the intentional fully conceives its limitations. "The gate / To the enclosure" becomes then the

42. Stevens, "Variations on a Summer Day," II.
43. See note 41.
44. "Of Mere Being."

opening into reality. And "the poem of the mind in the act of finding / What will suffice"[45] becomes the poem of the mind in the process of annihilating itself on the threshold of the natural perspective.

In "Un Coup de dès" Mallarmé recognizes, after a long and arduous attempt to arrive at the absolute form of the universe, that the absolute is itself subsumed within gratuitousness, and the poetic imagination is drowned by the reality it cannot master. In the last of the "Haiku" poems, though perhaps for different reasons, Seferis too denies the ontological success of the poetic act:

> You write:
> the ink grew less,
> the sea increases.[46]

Whether positively or negatively, the poetic act is placed in the past tense and engulfed by the present and the presence of a reality which it cannot order or contain. Wordsworth, Yeats, and Stevens ultimately assert the ontological primacy of reality against the human imagination, and their search for the poetic act that will suffice is equally a search for the act that will transport them beyond the intentional confines of their worlds, into the natural perspective from which they seem to be forever doomed to wander. Wordsworth accounts for his exile in terms of gain, and growth. Yeats affirms the historical process that destroys him and is surprised, at the end, to find that "what seemed hard / Should be so simple."[47] Stevens, more arduously and more lucidly than Yeats, regains the natural after a long struggle with the intentional: the poem of the mind, recognizing the limits of imagination, posits its inability to approach the object, and the moment of denial becomes the moment of revelation, the achievement of a transparence in which self and world are one.

45. Stevens, "Of Modern Poetry."
46. *Collected Poems,* p. 95.
47. "The Phases of the Moon."

❧ WORDSWORTH

There is a tradition in poetry in which the imagination appears as "the widow of an insight lost."[1] Poets who place ontological validity in the real world tend to see the imagination as both the vehicle for experiencing the natural and as an intruder in the world of things. The imagination arises when the oneness of self and world has been lost, when the experience of isolation has taken place. And its paradoxical function is to retrieve that initial vision whose loss gave it birth; to enter, through consciousness, a world from which all consciousness is excluded.

This tradition explains the importance, in Wordworth's poetry, of the figures of the child and the old man. They are symbols of a consciousness not yet born and a consciousness becoming dispersed, once more, into reality. In the early poetry in particular, the child figures signal precisely the absence of imagination, a oneness with the natural world. They are human figures unconscious of their humanity, inhabiting nature and dying into it before they can withdraw; sufficient, like the animals, unto themselves. Similarly the old men, so old that they are almost insentient, bespeak this growing proximity to the world of things.

These extremes of closeness to the natural point to the pervading sense of loss that informs some of Wordsworth's best poetry. The child who lives in the immediate reality of his world acquires,

1. Gerard Manley Hopkins, "To R. B."

in growing up, a consciousness of self which bars him from re-
entering the natural perspective. And the poet finds himself exiled
in a world which he can no longer see with the penetrating vision
of his youth. Exile and poetry, in fact, become synonymous, and
the attempt to transcend this isolation only serves to accentuate
the poles between which the dialectic operates. In *Les Rêveries du
promeneur solitaire,* Rousseau wishes to be "completely myself
and belonging to myself," and to "suffice myself like God."[2] To
accomplish this, he would have to abandon himself to the will of
nature ("to be what nature has willed"[3]) and at the same time
preserve the uniqueness of self which generates the wish for integration. The *Rêveries,* in fact, develop in terms of a struggle with
the very nature of artistic creation. The annihilation of the self
that occurs in the "rêverie" is opposed by the affirmation of the
self writing *about* the "rêverie." The ontologically valid experience and its aesthetic representation do not coincide. Like Rousseau, Wordsworth wishes to be both consciousness and reality—
at one with nature, but a witness to that union. He finds, of course,
that consciousness and reality are dialectical forces, and that the
attempt to synthesize them may endanger the act of poetry itself.
His early poems thus develop in terms of child protagonists clearly
distinguished from the poet, remaining or passing into the world
of nature while the poet bears witness to their passage from the
perspective of human time. Even in poems where the protagonist
is also the narrator the distinction between the experience and the
account of it remains.

This distinction between the "I" of the protagonist and the "I"
of the poet stems from, and in turn widens, the gap between nature and time. The valid experience for Wordsworth involves a
passage into the natural perspective, a merging of the self with the
objects it perceives. Yet what gives validity to this experience is

2. Jean-Jacques Rousseau, *Les Rêveries du promeneur solitaire* (Paris:
Garnier, 1960): "pleinement moi et à moi" ("Seconde promenade,"
p. 13) and "tant que cet état dure on se suffit à soi-même comme Dieu"
("Cinquième promenade," p. 71).
3. Seconde promenade," p. 13.

not its immediacy, its presentness, but precisely its place in the temporal perspective. Thus we note the curious use of "now" in relation to past tenses, and the constant thrusting of significant experiences into a past from which they may be neither truly lost nor truly recaptured. The Wordsworthian imagination seeks out the world of nature but validates it in the world of time, placing it in a context in which it can be "re-membered." It is of course the inescapable function of consciousness to constantly transform experience into memory. But in trying to place the experience of nature within a temporal order in which restoration is always possible, Wordsworth paradoxically casts it back into the alienating process of temporality. However, though the experience as experience is destroyed by the temporal perspective, it is simultaneously redeemed from oblivion by the very temporality which destroys it.

The affirmation of a relationship between human time and the natural perspective in turn makes possible Wordsworth's assertion that the act of creation is an integrative and not an alienating act, that the poet, in creating, works "in alliance" with the natural world. Imagination and nature are initially conceived to be "kindred streams," so that poetic creation becomes revelation of the real. Yet Wordsworth finds it difficult to sustain this conception. While in the retrospective vision of *The Prelude* he will continue to affirm this relationship of nature and poetry, in a more immediate context he will sense the tension between imagination and reality and validate his withdrawal from nature in terms of poetic survival: "with unobserving eye / Bent earthwards . . ." ("A Night-piece"). The eye bent earthwards is always the unobserving eye, the bodily eye caught in the visible scheme of things. Nature, the poet tells us, has held him in a "powerless trance," a trance which he must break in order to become "a creative soul." The "bodily eye"—"the most despotic of our senses"—is rejected for the "inward eye" and the visionary perspective. But the withdrawal from nature, which is initiated as a way of affirming the function of the poetic imagination, leads Wordsworth into a movement of ascension in which the imagination risks becoming self-consciously creative. The movement upward is also a movement inward, a recognition of the autonomy of the imagination which tends to disjoint the Wordsworthian image from its object and lead the imagination into a vision of transcendence that blinds the poet to the universe of things. The objects are infused with "light divine," but they have lost their solidity and their "thingness." Though Wordsworth is willing to conceive of nature and poetry to some extent in dialectical terms, he does not see any dialectic operating between the natural and the transcendent. Yet the dialectic is there.[4] The imagination that dissociates itself from nature and moves upward to achieve a vision of the transcendent becomes ultimately incapable of truly recovering the immediate relationship to the natural world.

Wordsworth of course does not accept this growing autonomy of imagination from nature as a fact. While on the one hand he will argue that the imagination must disengage itself from nature's sway, he will also suggest that the ascension of the imagination leads to a vision which contains both nature and the infinite, so that the transcendent and the immediate are not conceived in opposition to each other, but as part of the force that "rolls through all things." Yet the effects of this imaginative ascension make themselves felt. In "Tintern Abbey" the "sad perplexity" remains a barrier between the temporal and the natural worlds. Equally in *The Prelude* the "soulless image" suggests the inability of the poetic imagination to bring the disparate elements together in a pattern of unification and growth. In its movement upward and inward and in its validation of the temporal perspective the poetic imagination dissociates itself from the natural world it would regain and discovers itself the captive of a consciousness at odds with reality. The long-awaited dawn of being is repeatedly revealed as a false dawn.

Like most romantics, Wordsworth embarks on a quest for totality which is inimical to the immediate experience of the real. It takes almost a century for poetry to turn away from the desire for the

4. That it emerges in spite of Wordsworth's protestations to the contrary points to the authenticity of his poetry.

absolute and begin to affirm the specific object, the particular
truth, the delimited place. Yet it is also to Wordsworth's credit
that unlike most romantics he maintains the tenuous balance between imagination and reality without "falling upward" into
consciousness or drowning in the plenitude of things.[5]

The Sad Perplexity

The discrepancy between the temporal and the natural perspectives takes the form of a rift in the self between what it remembers
itself to have been and what it recognizes itself to be. Wordsworth so often looks at his childhood with the ambivalence of a
man who knows that there is no return and who is grateful for the
remembrance which both restores the past and forces upon him a
recognition of its pastness.

> A tranquillising spirit presses now
> On my corporeal frame, so wide appears
> The vacancy between me and those days
> Which yet have such self-presence in my mind,
> That, musing on them, often do I seem
> Two consciousnesses, conscious of myself
> And of some other Being. [*The Prelude*, II, 27–33]

Presence and absence are part of the poet's being-in-time, looking
at his past self and knowing that the rituals of entrance into nature are no longer valid. The boy in the skating scene (I, 452–
463) may elicit a movement of response from nature. The poet
recounting the experience evaluates it from the point of view of
time and remains conscious of its loss. *The Prelude* attempts to
overcome these two consciousnesses, to bind them in a pattern of
growth and self-recognition. But this too is the effort of the major
poems as well as the shorter lyrics—to bind together the disparate
selves created by time into the "natural piety" of a continuous
response.

5. Paul de Man refers to an "upward fall" in his essay on "Ludwig
Binswanger and the Sublimation of the Self," *Blindness and Insight* (New
York: Oxford University Press, 1971), p. 46.

"My heart leaps up" deals with this continuity of response to nature from the perspective of time, and the brevity of the poem makes the treatment of the problem—the poet's desire for this continuity of response—more striking. "My heart leaps up when I behold / A rainbow in the sky."[6] The poet's immediate perception of and response to the rainbow is placed by the third line within the context of duration: "So was it when my life began; / So is it now I am a man; / So be it when I shall grow old." This seems to be the recurrent structure of the Wordsworthian experience: to place the now—the instant of perception—within the context of temporality, to validate the moment of experience by perceiving it ultimately in the context of past and future, and therefore in its pastness. "Or let me die": death is conceived as the inability to perceive the object immediately, and simultaneously as a break in the continuity of perception and response. Temporal continuity thus becomes in Wordsworth part of a life-giving process. The "spots of time" do not stand alone. Without the backward glance and the widening temporal vision they would be lost in a morass of experience without meaning.

Within this temporal vision man grows and develops from his childhood perceptions. An essential, organic continuity between the child and the man is postulated here in terms of a continuing response to nature within the context of time: the child fathers the man. Yet we know that Wordsworth's later discoveries belie this statement, that self-recognition and maturity will lead him to an experience not of continuity, but of isolation. The "natural piety," which suggests a relation to nature of total acceptance and involvement, will turn into "the philosophic mind," "the feeling intellect," a relation in which the basic oneness of self and world

6. Perhaps the rainbow is a poor choice of natural object, since Wordsworth measures his distance from nature by his ability to respond to every "common sight": "There was a time when meadow, grove, and stream, / The earth, and every common sight, / To me did seem . . ." ("Ode: Intimations of Immortality"), and again, "It was, in truth, / An ordinary sight . . ." (The Prelude, XII, 253–254). See Hartman, The Unmediated Vision, p. 131.

will be compromised and perhaps irrevocably broken. "My heart leaps up" is a poem about growth, but from the point of view of the child, who can affirm with ease such continuity. From the point of view of the poet, growth will lead to isolation and estrangement. The poet will not be the protagonist of the poems on childhood, and indeed the child will die in order to sustain the unified vision in which he unconsciously lives.

In spite of Wordsworth's claim that it is possible—perhaps imperative—to establish a pattern of continuity between the child and the man, which in turn necessitates a very solid temporal perspective, we find that the child and the poet remain separate precisely over the issue of time and death. This separateness usually takes the form of a distinction between the poet as protagonist and the poet as narrator. The child, or the solitary figure, dies into nature or remains alien to the poet's conscious encounter. And nature and time remain two distinct realms that the poet's consciousness can never quite bridge.

Wordsworth tries, in a number of poems, to pass into the child's vision of nature and death. This attempt is perhaps most evident in the Lucy poems, where the poet begins with terror at the thought of death and ends with acceptance and affirmation. He passes, so to speak, from human time to natural time, from the mature vision to the child's perspective. In the first of the Lucy poems death is a divisive element. The poet sees death from the point of view of human time, and the strange fit of passion is the fear of separation from Lucy that death would bring. Yet it is something that happens to him—"what once to me befell"—and not to Lucy, as if the child-protagonist were from the beginning impervious to that which the poet fears. We have thus in the Lucy poems a circular structure not unlike that of Dante's *Comedy* or Hegel's *Phenomenology*, one in which the narrative elements of the beginning presume the knowledge acquired at the end.

Other elements in the poem point to the relationship of Lucy and nature. The dream of Lucy *is* a dream of nature: "In one of those sweet dreams I slept, / Kind Nature's gentlest boon." And

the awakening of the protagonist, accompanied by the sinking of
the moon, points to the passage from natural to human time, and
into the fear of finality and death. It may in fact be argued that
the dream of Lucy/Nature is interrupted by the protagonist's
thought of death. Human time breaks into the natural world, and
as in "Nutting" its intrusion wreaks destruction.

Yet Wordsworth shies away from the implications that systematically arise out of his poems. He is so often on the verge of stat-
ing an irreconcilable conflict between nature and consciousness.
But invariably he turns away from such conclusions and most
often postulates dubious solutions that do not really come to grips
with the issues at stake. Here, the poet refuses to accept the
thought of Lucy's death, dismissing it as a "wayward thought"
and concluding the poem in the conditional. He has not reached
Lucy, nor has he accepted the reality of her death, her temporal
finiteness. Lucy is part of nature, the poet is in time. He "thinks
of" her death and at the same time moves away from the terror
that that thought brings. We have here both a dismissal of the
thought of Lucy's death as a "wayward thought," a "fit of passion" that befell him and not Lucy, and the suggestion that the
thought of Lucy's death is Lucy's death itself—hence the cautious
approach "I will dare to tell." At the end of the poem, the dialectical relationship between nature and time has been firmly
established, but we find the protagonist just as firmly committed
to disregarding it.

Yet "She dwelt among the untrodden ways" entails a recognition of Lucy's death. The poet grasps the fact of Lucy's death
from the perspective of time, in which absence is real: "She lived
unknown, and few could know / When Lucy ceased to be." Again
the dialectical relationship between nature and time is in evidence
here: Lucy is placed in the context of nature, metaphorized as a
flower, a star, and viewed by the protagonist from the perspective
of time. Her death passes almost unnoticed, except by the poet.
But the progression from the first to the second poem is evident:
the poet has moved to an acceptance of the fact of her death,

while still viewing her death from a perspective which involves the ultimate alienation: "The difference to me."

In "I travelled among unknown men," the third of the Lucy poems,[7] Lucy begins to be associated with a realm which the poet can inhabit. We find here a parallel isolation of Lucy and the poet. Lucy lived "unknown," the poet has traveled "among unknown men." Of course, Lucy's isolation spells out her intimacy with nature; the poet's isolation suggests rootlessness, wandering, an inability to find significant space. But he begins in this poem to find significance in the English landscape. Boundaries—even national boundaries, though it is doubtful that any nationalistic feeling can be read into the poem—suggest specificity and containment. The protagonist's return to England seems to point to some closer relationship to the dead Lucy. More important, it suggests that the dead Lucy is a living presence, contained in a specific place, imbuing that place with her being. From the acceptance of the fact of Lucy's death, Wordsworth moves to a recognition of her living presence. " 'Tis past, that melancholy dream," and the romantic urge for voyage is transformed into an affirmation of the finite space.

There is, also in this poem, an attempt to perceive what Lucy has perceived: "And thine too is the last green field / That Lucy's eyes surveyed." Behind the desire for the finite space lies the desire for Lucy's unmediated perception of things.

Structurally, "Three years she grew" is perhaps the least felicitous of the Lucy poems. Thematically, it signals the poet's recognition of Lucy's total absorption in nature and his acceptance of her "death." Nature takes the initiative in this poem, and Lucy is portrayed as a natural object, a "thing" that grew in sun and

7. The 1800 edition of *Lyrical Ballads* contained four Lucy poems: "Strange fits of passion," "She dwelt among the untrodden ways," "A slumber did my spirit seal" and—placed elsewhere in the volume—"Three years she grew." A year later (April 1801) Wordsworth included a fifth one, "I travelled among unknown men," in a letter to Mary Hutchinson. See H. M. Margoliouth, *Wordsworth and Coleridge, 1795–1834* (New York: Oxford University Press, 1953), p. 52.

shower. Though nature's speech seems stilted, it is significant that nature, and not the poet, is the one to perceive Lucy as a natural thing. The poet's perception in "She dwelt among the untrodden ways" was not sufficient to root her in the realm of nature. Nature's speech here underlines the fact that Lucy is already in that realm, independently of the poet's thoughts, and that she must be viewed from that perspective. From nature's point of view, Lucy is a flower to be reabsorbed into the earth and fulfill the cyclical pattern. The references to Lucy as a natural object are profuse, and they point to a natural process in which death means only regeneration.

As Lucy dies into nature, nature infuses her with its "law and impulse." The processes are simultaneous. Closeness to nature implies intimacy with death—but natural death, death as regeneration. Through the first three poems, the protagonist has viewed death from the point of view of time, and therefore in terms of a process of disintegration. Here he begins to pass into the point of view of nature, he begins to accept death not merely as a fact to come to terms with but as a circular pattern of rebirth. The protagonist passes, through the Lucy poems, from the point of view of time and consciousness to the point of view (if such there be) of nature; and hence from the refusal to accept Lucy's death, and from grief over her death, to acceptance and affirmation: "And her's shall be the breathing balm, / And her's the silence and the calm / Of mute insensate things." Instead of moving into the world of consciousness and divisiveness, Lucy sinks back into the world she already inhabits, and the poet-protagonist affirms her impenetrable objectivity, her "in-itselfness" and her silence. Her insentience, in fact, is the condition of her "presence." She responds immediately to the objects in reality, but as it were from the point of view of reality itself.

Yet the affirmation of Lucy as a part of nature is not complete. It is affirmed as a fact, but not validated by the protagonist. At the end of the poem, he is still grieving, still feeling her absence in spite of his affirmation of her natural presence, still looking at nature from the point of view of time. The paradox, of course, is that if the poet is to pass fully into the point of view of nature he will cease being a poet, a problem which Keats understands fully in "Ode to a Nightingale," but which Wordsworth systematically evades. The alternative is to make a distinction between protagonist and poet, but that too is a possibility that Wordsworth does not wish to entertain. At the end of the poem, the poet has not shaken off the point of view of consciousness. He still sees Lucy's death from within the temporal perspective, in which "what has been" is also what "never more will be." Lucy dead is Lucy absent from the linearly conceived world of time—absent because what has been exists in memory and points to the impossibility of its future recurrence.

It is finally in "A slumber did my spirit seal" that the poet moves more fully into the perspective of nature and overcomes his grief:

> A slumber did my spirit seal;
> I had no human fears:
> She seemed a thing that could not feel
> The touch of earthly years.

Lucy's insentience is here reiterated. She seems a "thing," and in the measure in which she is a natural object she escapes the movement of time: "Rolled round in earth's diurnal course, / With rocks, and stones, and trees." She is motionless, yet moves with the cycles of nature, with the "law and impulse" of nature herself. She is dead, but a living presence, unable to perceive reality because she is reality itself. Lucy dead is Lucy both alive and asleep in nature, and the sleep she sinks into is one finally shared by the protagonist. The slumber that seals the spirit of the poet also allows him to pass into a vision of nature that transforms his perception of time. We see him go, through the five poems, from " 'O mercy!' to myself I cried, / 'If Lucy should be dead!' " to "I had no human fears," from the dismissal of the wayward thought to acceptance, and to more than acceptance, validation. In the first poem Wordsworth feared the possibility of Lucy's death viewed from the perspective of time. Here, he has no *human* fears; he disengages himself from the temporal perspective and accepts more fully the point of view of nature. He passes, so to speak, into Lucy's unconscious and unmediated perception of reality. The slumber, too, suggests this letting go of human time. It takes us back to the "sweet dream" of the first poem, which was "kind Nature's gentlest boon." The slumber is a dream of nature and of Lucy, by which the poet transcends the purely human perspective. Through slumber, he passes from one point of view to the other and transcends the limitations of consciousness and the finiteness of the temporal. Finally, slumber also "seals" the spirit of the poet, granting it this larger perspective and healing his grief and fear of temporality and death.[8]

Yet it is in this poem that the question of the relationship of poet and protagonist might well be raised. Were the poet to pass fully into the realm of nature, the imagination would not be so much "naturalized" as destroyed, dissolved into the cyclical pattern of rocks and stones and trees. What inevitably "saves" the poetic imagination from perdition is the fact that the poet recounts an experience that has taken place in the past. Though the theme of the Lucy poems may be the transition from the temporal to the natural perspective, the very structure, the very existence of these poems goes counter to their theme and points to the poet's grounding in the world of time. This grounding is underlined by Wordsworth's deliberate use of the past tense, which keeps the poetic imagination from annihilation but also prevents it from becoming a rite of passage into nature. This is the paradoxical relationship, in so many of Wordsworth's poems, between nature and imagination. The protagonist (or narrator-in-the-poem) of the Lucy poems may fall into a slumber of nature, but the poet

8. See Hartman's reading of the Lucy poems in terms of voice in *The Fate of Reading*, pp. 161–162, 291. See also de Man's reading of "A slumber did my spirit seal" in terms of the "actual temporality of the experience" and the "ideal, self-created temporality engendered by the language of the poem" in "The Rhetoric of Temporality," *Interpretation: Theory and Practice*, pp. 173–209, particularly pp. 205–206.

recounts this experience of sleep from the point of view of wakefulness, and time.[9]

The relationship between nature and time is most clearly explored in two poems—"There was a Boy" and "Tintern Abbey."

> There was a Boy; ye knew him well, ye cliffs
> And islands of Winander!

The poem opens in the past tense, pointing to the fact that a remembered experience is once again the subject of the poem. After the abrupt opening "there was a boy," Wordsworth goes on to establish the relationship between the boy and the natural world. The cliffs and the islands "knew him well," as if a separate consciousness dwelt within nature—a consciousness which could, like the cliffs in the skating scene of Book I of *The Prelude,* respond to the child's movement toward oneness.

There is, in fact, a similar event in this poem: a oneness achieved not through movement and visual response, but through sound. The child blows "mimic hootings to the silent owls," and the owls—and the natural world—are "responsive to his call." The response of the natural world is overwhelming, its "generosity" far exceeding the movement outward on the part of the child. In the answer to the child's call are mingled the owls' response and the echo of the original call, until the mimic hooting and the echo, the echo and the response, become one vast encompassing movement of unity.

Following this profusion of sound comes a sudden moment of vacancy in nature: "And, when there came a pause / Of silence such as baffled his best skill. . . . " But just as suddenly the vacancy becomes the vehicle for a more than natural experience. In Book VI of *The Prelude* the light of sense goes out and in the process reveals an invisible world (600–602). In "There was a Boy" the harmony becomes manifest through the absence of

---

9. A similar paradox operates in Keats's "Sleep and Poetry," where the poet, awake, writes about sleep and in the morning is "surprised . . . from a sleepless night."

sound. As this happens, the child is "surprised"; he is confronted with a reality that has come into the natural scene and yet is one that has always been there. The sudden absence in reality has revitalized its presence. And it enters "unawares" into the mind of the boy, to be stored and later recollected by the poet.

The significant experience, however, takes place in the second stanza, where the poet stands apart both from the events recounted in the first stanza and, at the same time, from his past self. We know, from an early version of the poem as well as from its place in *The Prelude,* that Wordsworth is indeed the child. Yet the child's death "ere he was full twelve years old" creates a distinction between narrator and protagonist and establishes a profound temporal discontinuity. The child in this case is not the "father of the man." Like Lucy, he dies into nature, thrusting the poet's conscious self into the temporal perspective.

> This boy was taken from his mates, and died
> In childhood, ere he was full twelve years old.
> Pre-eminent in beauty is the vale
> Where he was born and bred: the church-yard hangs
> Upon a slope above the village-school;
> And, through that churchyard when my way has led
> On summer-evenings, I believe that there
> A long half-hour together I have stood
> Mute—looking at the grave in which he lies!

The poet, at the end, stands by the grave of his past self. Yet the discontinuity exists not only within the temporal perspective—the disruption of past and present, the child and the man—but also between the temporal and the natural worlds. These are, of course, two aspects of a single problem, given the child's relationship to nature in Wordsworth's poetry. The poet looks at the child's grave from the point of view of time and in it sees not the boy's oneness with nature—as he does in the Lucy poems—but temporal finiteness, and death. Simultaneously, in looking at the boy's grave, the poet-protagonist looks at his past self and recognizes its pastness. The recognition of the disjunction between past and present selves leads to a paradoxical simultaneity of muteness and speech: the protagonist stands mute, the poet writes the poem about muteness and dissociation. The discontinuity between nature and time spells the poet's incapacity to recollect himself in the temporal perspective. Though memory supposedly brings the self together into a cogent identity, it also forces upon the poet a consciousness of temporality which separates him from the natural world, or underlines the already existing separation. The remembrance thus turns into an act of dismembering. Memory brings him "together," but memory also makes him conscious of his irrevocable separation from the boy, and of the grave that lies in nature as a symbol of time.[10]

"Nutting" presents a similar clash between the temporal and the natural worlds, though less forcefully than "There was a Boy." The protagonist recounts here his boyhood experience, one which symbolically focuses on the passage from childhood to maturity, from oneness with nature to consciousness of self, and from the natural to the temporal world. The child comes upon a place untouched by the human world. Yet there is already in the boy the incipience of consciousness. Less at one with nature than Lucy, whose imminent death places her perhaps in a privileged position, the boy recognizes his perception of nature and his feeling of joy. Perhaps, of course, the poet recognizes it for him in after-meditation. Such recognition—and the incipient consciousness it points to—make inevitable what follows. The child destroys the natural scene and passes into the conscious, temporal world. The narrative of the poem is of course complicated by the fact that the poet is recounting the boy's feelings from the point of view of time, so that the temporal perspective is all-pervading and the passage from nature into time inevitable. Wordsworth tells us that he may "confound" his present feelings with the past. That such confusion is possible points to the simultaneous success and failure of the poetic vision: it is successful in moving back in time and

10. See Geoffrey H. Hartman's reading of this poem in *Wordsworth's Poetry 1787–1814* (New Haven: Yale University Press, 1964), pp. 19–22, and also his later reading in *The Fate of Reading*, pp. 183, 286, 289–291.

recognizing the feelings of the child, establishing thus a continuity in the self, but unsuccessful in binding together the temporal and the natural perspectives. For the poem to take place nature has to give up "her quiet being." The passage we witness from childhood to maturity and the accompanying split between natural and human time are precisely what make the poem possible. The poem thus meditates on the inevitable destruction of the natural which ultimately allows the poetic act to take place but which the poem paradoxically wishes to transcend.

It is perhaps in "Tintern Abbey" that Wordsworth explores most clearly and most profoundly the relationship of the temporal and the natural worlds:

> Five years have past; five summers, with the length
> Of five long winters! and again I hear
> These waters, rolling from their mountain-springs
> With a soft inland murmur.—Once again
> Do I behold these steep and lofty cliffs,
> That on a wild secluded scene impress
> Thoughts of more deep seclusion; and connect
> The landscape with the quiet of the sky.

The perspective of time—"five years have past"—yields almost immediately to the perspective of nature—"five summers, with the length / Of five long winters." Nature repeats itself in time, it escapes the temporal finiteness of the human: "again I hear . . . once again do I behold . . . I again repose . . . once again I see." Of course, these phrases center not on nature but on the perceiving self, and in a sense point to the problem the poem will contend with. But at the outset the temporal seems to be overwhelmed by the natural, both by the repetition of "again" and the redundant use of adjectives and nouns with the same stem. These suggest continuity and permanence and point to the poet's ability to return to a particular place and a particular moment in time.

> These beauteous forms,
> Through a long absence, have not been to me
> As is a landscape to a blind man's eye.

We have in this poem a curious superimposition of remembrances. We find, of course, what we suspected: that Wordsworth is not writing the poem in the presence of the scene. The present tense of the beginning is misleading, and it soon moves into the past tense of the poem as a whole. But within this poetic past tense the presentness of the landscape leads the poet to remember the landscape in its absence. He remembers his remembrance of the landscape and tries to connect it to its "presence" in the beginning of the poem and to a less distant memory of the scene. The absent scene has sustained its presence in the mind and given birth to "unremembered pleasure," pleasure abstracted from the recollection rather than from the experience, unremembered because it occurs only after the experience is past. Wordsworth is indeed far more conscious of nature in its absence, and pleasure is invariably brought forth not directly from the natural scene but from its confrontation with the world of time. What generates this pleasure, of course, is also what poses the problem. But in this passage nature and memory work together in a process of healing and growth. The presence of nature within the temporal perspective is devoid of any tension here, and makes possible a "tranquil restoration."

> Until, the breath of this corporeal frame
> And even the motion of our human blood
> Almost suspended, we are laid asleep
> In body, and become a living soul:
> While with an eye made quiet by the power
> Of harmony, and the deep power of joy,
> We see into the life of things.

In previous poems there was a strong suggestion that the natural perspective was valid in and for itself, and human time was associated to some extent with destructiveness and isolation. We find in "Tintern Abbey" that human time is the vehicle of growth and that nature is less the "all in all," less the realm of being. The wholeness of being is to be achieved not by a transcendence of time but by a "beyonding" of nature. In this sense "Tintern Abbey" is the turning point from Wordsworth's affirmation of nature to his validation of the transcendent. Though he stresses here the value of both, we find that the memory of nature is in "Tintern Abbey" associated no longer with an attempt to return to an immediate world, but precisely with the opposite, a movement away from the visible. Nature is of course the realm of the immediate, but the memory of nature functions in Wordsworth as a force of transcendence. It makes the poet see into things, as he says, but also through them. The corporeal frame is forgotten in order to give way to the living soul. The "bodily eye" that holds the child in a "powerless trance" becomes in "Tintern Abbey" the "eye made quiet" that transcends the visible scene and intuits nature in its absence—often, as here, remembering the remembrance rather than the presence. The eye made quiet is thus the eye of memory, which draws the poet away from present and presence to let him see "into the life of things." Wordsworth's claim, of course, is that the act of seeing *into* things links him even more profoundly to the natural world. Memory and nature, in other words the temporal and the natural perspectives, are not conceived in opposition, but are inextricably linked.

> And now, with gleams of half-extinguished thought,
> With many recognitions dim and faint,
> And somewhat of a sad perplexity,
> The picture of the mind revives again.

In terms of the relationship between nature and time, this is the center if not the turning point of the poem. With the words "and now," the poet moves back into the "present tense" within the poem, that is, into the temporal perspective, while ostensibly viewing the natural landscape. This slight distance introduced into the unity which had so far been established between the temporal and the natural slowly widens as the passage progresses. The protagonist confronts the visible scene with his memory of the scene, and instead of the movement of connectedness and fusion we have found so far in the poem, the natural and the remembered are separated by the "sad perplexity." The picture of the scene preserved by memory within the temporal perspective does not flow into the visible scene. Indeed, it points to a disjunc-

tion between memory and nature which the poet's philosophical
arguments will try to explain but which they will not fully overcome.

Yet Wordsworth brushes off the "sad perplexity," refuses to
give it weight. The lines that follow this passage suggest that,
sincerely or not, the poet is beginning to come to terms with this
disjunction between the temporal and the natural:

> While here I stand, not only with the sense
> Of present pleasure, but with pleasing thoughts
> That in this moment there is life and food
> For future years.

That he can remember the past scene at all is pleasurable in itself,
but to this fact he adds his ability to remember the "present"
scene in the future. Once again, we see the poet abstracting himself from the presence of nature, grounding himself in a temporal
perspective in which the act of cognition is invariably one of
recognition and in which the disparities between memory and
nature can be explained in terms of growth.[11]

To account for this growth, the protagonist moves back to his
boyhood days, explaining the difference between then and now
and validating both the loss and the gain. In the past, we are told,
nature was "all in all":

> —I cannot paint
> What then I was. The sounding cataract
> Haunted me like a passion.

Wordsworth places this relationship irrevocably in the past and
moves to affirm a different relation with nature:

> —That time is past,
> And all its aching joys are now no more,

11. This recognition sometimes takes the form of a confusion of past
and present feelings, of thoughts arrived at during the experience and
thoughts "unremembered," arrived at in "after-meditation": "and, unless
I now / Confound my present feelings with the past . . ." (Nutting")
or "I cannot say what portion is in truth / The naked recollection of that
time, / And what may rather have been called to life / By after-meditation" (*The Prelude,* III, 613–616).

> And all its dizzy raptures. Not for this
> Faint I, nor mourn nor murmur; other gifts
> Have followed; for such loss, I would believe,
> Abundant recompense.

From the time in which nothing was "unborrowed from the eye,"
we have passed into the time of the quiet eye, in which a scene is
abstracted and remembered, and ultimately recognized. Memory
in Wordsworth functions as a force of abstraction, of withdrawal
from the immediacy of nature. But it works also as a force of
fruition, bringing the self into a kind of stasis and measuring
growth. In "My heart leaps up" the ability to respond contin-
uously to nature was the life-giving element, the "natural piety."
In "Tintern Abbey" the poet recognizes that the response has
changed. Thus it is no longer the sameness in response that binds
days each to each in natural piety, but the memory that recollects
the experience without regaining it and accounts for change, as
we have said, in terms of growth. The element of continuity is to
be found no longer in nature, but in time.[12] Perhaps this shift explains Wordsworth's contention that love of nature has led to love
of man. This new relationship to nature is based on the poet's
being anchored in the world of time. To see nature be it in terms
of loss or gain is to see it not for itself but in terms of human time.
The sense of immediacy is lost, but then nature is humanized.

If memory is indeed abstractive in Wordsworth, we can see
how it is at the same time creative. The protagonist withdraws
from the scene in order to truly harvest it. And as he does he infuses the purely natural with human meaning.

> Therefore I am still
> A lover of the meadows and the woods,
> And mountains; and of all that we behold
> From this green earth; of all the mighty world
> Of eye, and ear,—both what they half create,
> And what perceive.

The senses are transcended, so that what they perceive is not only

12. We should point out here that "Tintern Abbey" was composed in
1798, "My heart leaps up" in 1802.

what is perceptible, but also what is remembered and validated. Nature is transformed from "all in all" to "the guardian of my heart, and soul / Of all my moral being," from the force that held him in a "powerless trance" to a nurse that "never did betray / The heart that loved her." It is there, but seen now from the perspective of time.

This temporal perspective is solidified in the last part of the poem by the presence of Dorothy. Dorothy is an image—a symbol —of the past, a reflecting surface that gives him back his past and at the same time allows him to transcend it. She is "the language of [his] former heart." "Oh! yet a little while / May I behold in thee what I was once." The disjunction between nature and time brought forth by the sad perplexity at the disconnection between the remembered and the visible has been to some extent overcome. "Other gifts / Have followed." But it is Dorothy that seems to truly link these two worlds, these two disjointed perspectives, binding the poet's days each to each in natural piety. We see her first as a figure of memory, containing and reflecting Wordsworth's past. Then we see her in her relation to nature—"when thy mind / Shall be a mansion for all lovely forms, / Thy memory be as a dwelling-place / For all sweet sounds and harmonies." We then see her projected into the future, having transcended, like Wordsworth, the immediacy with nature, but retaining a relationship to it in a different form, a relationship bound up with Wordsworth's presence. Dorothy is the great force of continuity in the poem not because she is a figure of memory, but because she stands between the remembered and the visible, the temporal and the natural, a human figure in a dissolving world.

At the same time, the poet sees in Dorothy the same process of growth through which he has already passed, so that she is a "stage" in his development, temporally prior to his, and therefore closer to nature. Just as she stands between him and nature, she also stands between him and his former self. At the end of the poem, the protagonist exhorts her to "remember" her relation to nature and his own relation both to nature and to her. Through

her, he establishes and solidifies links between the temporal and
the natural, links supposedly created by the very act of writing
the poem. He asks her to remember his own relation to nature,
his own encounter with past and present, and her own presence—
all these events both in the poem and exterior to the poem, giving
rise to the poem but contained within the poem itself. He asks
her, in fact, to remember his own act of remembrance which gave
birth to the poem. To create this kind of parallel between Dorothy
and the poetic act is to see poetry, as we know Wordsworth does,
as a process of fusion, binding the dialectical forces of nature and
time in a process of tranquil restoration.

The process of abstractiveness that we saw fleetingly in "Tintern
Abbey" returns in "I wandered lonely as a cloud" and becomes in
fact the central experience of the poem. The poet begins by seeing
a host of golden daffodils from the perspective of a cloud, and at
the end of the poem reveals what is significant about the experience:

> For oft, when on my couch I lie
> In vacant or in pensive mood,
> They flash upon that inward eye
> Which is the bliss of solitude.

The perspective of temporal distance established at the end of the
poem has its counterpart in the spatial distance of the beginning.
Though Wordsworth claims that he wishes to keep his eye on the
object, though he tells us that his wish is to relate to the particular
and the specific in nature, the first stanza establishes what is a
typical approach to the visible scene in his poetry: seeing the
object, or the conglomeration of objects, from a spatial and temporal distance that makes the poet's view more encompassing.
The initial isolation of the poet—"lonely as a cloud"—is quickly
forgotten in the act of perception that follows. And the simile link-
ing the poet to a natural object contains his isolation within the
natural perspective.

The second stanza establishes a continuity of perspective by
comparing the daffodils to the stars: "Continuous as the stars

that shine." Once again this continuity of perception places the poet at the center of his vision rather than at a point from which all becomes invisible or intangible, and in this sense assimilates him to the objects he perceives. The cloud finds itself surrounded by daffodils-stars, and the horizontal and the vertical dimensions are indistinguishable.

Yet again we may argue that relating to ten thousand daffodils is different from relating to a single object in a world that rapidly eludes him. Wordsworth will recognize this in the "Intimations Ode" and bemoan his inability to experience the single tree, the single field. In "I wandered lonely as a cloud," however, the spatial perspective is affirmed and validated by the perspective of time introduced at the end of the fourth stanza. The withdrawal from and meditation on the experience is precisely what constitutes the valid experience of the poem. Once again it is not the "bodily eye" or the direct sensory perception which the poet seeks, but the "inward eye" which is the vision of memory. The act of insight and the act of remembrance are here simultaneous. The significant experience occurs not in direct contact with nature, but in the recollection that takes place in time and validates the previous encounter. As will be the case with the "Intimations Ode," the movement inward which makes possible a vision (a "re-presentation") of absent things depends on and in turn reaffirms the perspective of time in which the poem is grounded. What is gained—the ability to recollect at will—far exceeds the loss of the immediate perception and the initial experience.

The attempt to regain the natural perspective thus takes the form in Wordsworth of a reliance on memory which in turn affirms the temporal perspective. In fact, the remembered becomes far more valid than the immediate, because it allows for a continuity and a sense of self which oneness with nature would preclude.

> How I have stood, to fancies such as these
> A stranger, linking with the spectacle
> No conscious memory of a kindred sight,

> And bringing with me no peculiar sense
> Of quietness or peace.   [*The Prelude,* I, 572–576]

Cognition of the natural object is superseded, in terms of ontological value, by recognition. Without remembrance, there seems
to be a dismembering of the self in time. The function of memory
in Wordsworth is to provide this force of continuity between disparate selves in time, and in so doing to bridge the radically different perspectives of the self into a process of growth and restoration. The recollection of the past experience is thus in the fullest
meaning of the term a harvesting, a gathering-in of the temporally
splintered self into fruition, and quietness and peace.

> Even then I felt
> Gleams like the flashing of a shield;—the earth
> And common face of Nature spake to me
> Rememberable things.   [*The Prelude,* I, 585–588]

Wordsworth will see in nature not the "in-itselfness" of the real,
but what is "rememberable": not the object itself, but the inter-
action between self and object that binds the natural and the
temporal in the vision of the inward eye.

This affirmation of the inward eye is also a paradoxical affirmation of something permanent in a changing world. Wordsworth
speaks in *The Prelude* of "a Power" that

> Holds up before the mind intoxicate
> With present objects, and the busy dance
> Of things that pass away, a temperate show
> Of objects that endure.   [XIII, 29–32]

The immediate experience involves a dissolving of the self in the
natural perspective, an intoxication of the self with the present
and the presence of things, in short, a forgetfulness of self. Identity
can only be affirmed within time, and thus the force of memory
which was allied with the inner vision of the daffodils becomes
also an affirmation of the temporal world which both prohibits
the poet's passage into nature and allows him at the same time
to recollect such passages. The dissolving of the self in the im-

mediate is discarded here, transcended rather, for the affirmation of the self in terms of the temporal and the enduring. The paradox lies in the simultaneous affirmation of the temporal perspective which isolates the poet from nature and the quest for the enduring which can be found only in the temporal world. Yet it is a paradox presumably synthesized, or transcended, by a movement backward in time which contains past and present and a movement of ascension into a more encompassing transcendent world.

"Tintern Abbey" offers perhaps the most viable, least strained resolution to the dialectical relationship of nature and time. Wordsworth returns to the problem in the "Intimations Ode," but there the answers seem less felicitous.

"Tintern Abbey" opens with a statement of the continuity between the temporal and the natural. The "Intimations Ode" opens with a statement of a break between them. Though the epigraph from "My heart leaps up" points to Wordsworth's attempt to once again bind his days "each to each by natural piety," the opening of the "Ode" returns to the problem of a qualitative difference in the poet's perception of nature:

> There was a time when meadow, grove, and stream,
> The earth, and every common sight,
>   To me did seem
>   Apparelled in celestial light,
> The glory and the freshness of a dream.

"The rainbow comes and goes," and his heart does not leap up. Yet a new element has been introduced into the "Ode": nature, at the time when his perception of it was immediate, was "apparelled in celestial light," clothed, as he will say later, in a glory not its own.[13] In the opening of the "Ode" the poet is laying the groundwork for an explanation of his sense of loss, an explanation in which nature will cease having the ontological primacy it has held until now. The implications of the argument are fairly clear even in the first stanza: if the immediacy of perception and response is due to nature's being clothed in celestial light, then what

13. See *The Prelude*, V, 605.

is at issue in the poem is the loss of that light, and not the poet's or the child's past ability to perceive things immediately. The dialectical relationship operates no longer between nature and time, but between the temporal and the transcendent, a dialectic far easier to synthesize philosophically than that between the temporal and the natural. Simultaneously, the problem of the protagonist is no longer posed as a loss of perception, but of vision. The particular object and the particular place are important only insofar as they partake of this celestial light. Perception of the natural is incidental to the vision of the transcendent.

> —But there's a Tree, of many, one,
> A single Field which I have looked upon,
> Both of them speak of something that is gone:
> The Pansy at my feet
> Doth the same tale repeat:
> Whither is fled the visionary gleam?
> Where is it now, the glory and the dream?

Because the visionary gleam has fled, not faded,[14] the continuity sought in the epigraph can be achieved only by a passage from immanence to transcendence, from the tangible to the invisible, and from experience to conceptualization. We see this happening from the fifth stanza on, where the platonic notion of memory is applied to perception. Thus the link between the child and nature is posited not in terms of immediacy or unconsciousness, but in terms of a transcendent element—the celestial light. *Because* the child remembers the celestial light, and is like nature clothed by it, he "vizionizes" nature. But also *because* the poet remembers or posits this transcendent reality, he is less able to relate to nature. Transcendence (the celestial light) is viewed here as a link between the child and the natural world. But transcendence also spells the poet's inability to relate to that world. The poetic imagination directs itself here to an elusive vision rather than a particular object, and it cannot feel the overpowering sense of presence without feeling at the same time the unimportance of

14. See Bloom, *The Visionary Company*, pp. 166–167.

the object itself. The power to "commune with the invisible world" (*The Excursion*, IX, 86) is translated into an incapacity to commune with the world of nature.

We are therefore not surprised to find in the sixth stanza that nature begins to be associated not with remembrance, as it was in "Tintern Abbey," but with forgetfulness. Nature loses here its ontological validity and becomes a pitfall, holding the poet in a powerless trance and making him forget the initial vision. In the measure in which nature is associated with forgetfulness and sleep, the poet's distance from nature becomes the valid form of remembrance. And the transcendence of nature becomes, as in "Tintern Abbey" but for different reasons, the means toward poetic vision. The survival of the poet, in fact, is seen in terms of his ability to distance himself from nature and view things from the perspective of transcendence. The vision of the transcendent and the perception of the particular have become mutually exclusive.

There are other implications to this change in Wordsworth's view of the relationship of nature and vision. In the early poetry he associates his ability to create with his ability to perceive immediately. Nature and imagination work "in alliance." As vision and perception become distinct, the ability to write poetry is in direct relationship to the poet's ability to distance himself from nature and see beyond it, into the life of things perhaps, but more obviously into the heart of a disembodied vision. Though Wordsworth shies away from this kind of argument, the implications are unavoidable. Nature and imagination are at odds with each other, and this feeling—whether a genuine one or the rationalization of a previous loss—paves the way for the withdrawal of the poetic imagination from natural reality, its ascension into a transcendent, invisible realm, and the concomitant devaluation and desacralization of the natural world. Ironically, it is as the soul frees itself from nature's sway that the sleep and the forgetting truly set in. The celestial light darkens the natural landscape, and the passage from immanence to transcendence, supposedly effected for the survival of poetry, paradoxically forces upon the poet a vision which blinds him to the world of things.

Wordsworth of course does not deal with these implications. If the poet in "Tintern Abbey" had to abstract himself from the visible scene in order to bring together the memory and the landscape, the temporal and the natural, he has here to break his ties to nature with even more finality, in order to come closer to the transcendent light which in the course of the poem has been given ontological validity. Memory in the "Ode" is no longer a specific remembrance of an experience of nature, but a force of transcendence that helps the poet break through the trappings of the visible and reach the source of things. The eye made quiet of "Tintern Abbey" points in the "Ode" to a placeless place in which memory and vision are one.

Wordsworth thus passes in the "Ode" from seeing memory in its relation to time to seeing it in its relation to eternity. Memory —because it is no longer a personal memory of past events—becomes a force not of temporality, but of transcendence and immortality.

> O joy! that in our embers
> Is something that doth live,
> That nature yet remembers
> What was so fugitive!

The embers—the consciousness of mortality—are superseded by the recognition of immortality through the very memory that is by definition grounded in time. The poet in fact tells us that he is thankful for the "obstinate questionings / Of sense and outward things" that have led him away from nature and into this vision of transcendence. The questioning begins as a movement of distance and ends as a movement of affirmation.

In the tenth stanza Wordsworth picks up images from previous stanzas, and though he qualifies his response to these natural objects ("we *in thought* will join your throng . . . "—my italics), he reiterates as in "Tintern Abbey" the fact that other gifts have followed: "We will grieve not, rather find / Strength in what remains behind." Instead of seeing past and future disjointed, as he did in the Lucy poems ("The memory of what has been, / And never more will be"), he sees them as continuous ("Which having been must ever be"). The intimations of immortality stem from the recognition of time and of mortality, from breaking the spell of nature "and all its dizzy raptures." At the end of the poem, the poet affirms his ability to be "moved" by "the meanest flower that blows." The response sought after by "My heart leaps up" is no longer accessible to him. Yet his days are indeed bound each to each by a different kind of piety, more mature, more philosophic.

Perhaps the last stanza, in which Wordsworth attempts to strengthen the resolution begun in the tenth stanza, brings out most poignantly the poet's loss. "I only have relinquished one delight / To live beneath your more habitual sway," he tells the natural objects which once held for him the quality of experiences. These objects have now ceased to be moments of experience; they have become, precisely, objects, closed within themselves, infinitely distant. And the poet who had claimed to reject the "powerless trance" of a too-potent nature now unwillingly but inescapably relinquishes his hold on these isolated moments. Not that he wills to let them go. He has no choice. But in asserting that it is good that they have gone, he irrevocably transforms his world.

> The innocent brightness of a new-born Day
>   Is lovely yet;
> The Clouds that gather round the setting sun
> Do take a sober colouring from an eye
> That hath kept watch o'er man's mortality.

Within the context of the transcendent light the poet can accept the present darkness of the rising and setting sun, the loss of his immediate relationship to nature, and the failure of his power to intuit the presence of objects. But it is precisely this transcendent quality of the light which destroys the possibility of immediacy, and the conceptualization from which it springs and which sustains it adds to the opacity of an already darkened world. The "sober colouring" is the coloring of spatial dispossession. As the conceptual imagination and the "inward eye" gain ground in Wordsworth's universe, the dark light of transcendence destroys the ontological primacy of the natural object and with it the experiential richness of the poetry itself.

Kindred Streams

The subservience of both nature and time to a celestial light in the "Intimations Ode" dispelled if not synthesized their dialectical relationship. In *The Prelude* the vision of the imagination takes on the role played by the celestial light in the "Ode," and the poet attempts to connect the perception of nature and the vision of the transcendent through the act of poetry itself. Though the vision of the transcendent encompasses both poetry and nature, it is the act of writing *The Prelude* that connects the disparate elements and reaches the ultimate revelation. *The Prelude* shows us the mind of the poet in the act of perceiving and interpreting the growth he has undergone. It is not surprising that the reverse is true—that the writing of *The Prelude* is itself what constitutes the growth of the poet's mind. The act of creation creates the creator.

The Prelude contains—and to some extent resolves—the problems dealt with in the Lucy poems, "Tintern Abbey," indeed the "Intimations Ode." Wordsworth presents here what he has lost and what he has gained in an all-encompassing view of poetic growth, and the historical, temporal perspective—the containment of his past, as it were—becomes a "cure" of the self from its feeling of loss and dispossession. The temporalizing tendency in Wordsworth's poetry in this sense grants him a more infinite perspective, and the necessary withdrawal from past experiences allows a meditation on the experience and on the larger context in which it is placed. Within the context of this temporal perspective, Wordsworth's meditations on childhood experiences always point to something beyond themselves. Rooted in the past, they transcend their temporal limitation and are woven into a pattern of growth and restoration.

This restoration and growth depend to some extent on the poet's ability to maintain a balance between nature and imagination, walking the narrow ridge between them without drowning into reality or "falling upward" into consciousness. But the notion of self-consciousness does not really enter *The Prelude*. Wordsworth maintains, except on brief occasions, that he creates "in alliance" with nature, that the act of poetry is an integrative, not an alienating act. In Book I, the "correspondent breeze" sets the tone for this sustained interchange:

> For I, methought, while the sweet breath of heaven
> Was blowing on my body, felt within
> A correspondent breeze, that gently moved
> With quickening virtue, but is now become
> A tempest, a redundant energy,
> Vexing its own creation.   [33–38]

Whatever feelings emerge in the self, they correspond to what already exists in nature, so that any discovery within the self points to a renewed contact with the outside world. The correspondent breeze within the self may, as Hartman suggests,[15] vex itself into creation, but its creation is always a discovery, a revelation that strengthens the bonds of the poet to "existing things." When Wordsworth speaks in Book II of the creativity of the child, the implication is that such creativity is not lost but rediscovered in the poet, who creates "creator and receiver both, / Working but in alliance with the works / Which it beholds" (258–260). The creative act in Wordsworth is sustained by, and in turn affirms, this alliance of mind and nature. And poetry is not problematic in the sense that it will be for Yeats or Stevens because it stems from the recognition of a relationship and consequently underscores that relationship. The act of perception is an act of creation in this passage not because it transforms as in Stevens the object perceived, but precisely because it reveals the object in terms of the self's relationship to it. In Book VI, the metaphor of the breeze is restated in terms of a stream that flows into a kindred stream:

15. *The Unmediated Vision,* p. 12.

>   Finally, whate'er
>   I saw, or heard, or felt, was but a stream
>   That flowed into a kindred stream; a gale,
>   Confederate with the current of the soul,
>   To speed my voyage.   [742–746]

Poetic creation and natural movement are a single act. The influx
of nature in the poet's mind—reminiscent of nature entering
"unawares" into the mind of the boy of Winander—is actually a
movement outward on the part of the poet, a movement that
"fits" him to "existing things." The workings of the mind are described in terms of natural imagery, and the singleness of purpose
created by this simultaneity of mind and nature speeds the poet's
voyage. The vision of the imagination, earlier in the book (in the
1805 version), has the opposite effect: it halts the progress of
his song.

>   Imagination! lifting up itself
>   Before the eye and progress of my Song
>   Like an unfather'd vapour; here that Power,
>   In all the might of its endowments, came
>   Athwart me; I was lost as in a cloud,
>   Halted, without a struggle to break through.   [VI, 592–597]

The passage quoted earlier, which occurs later in the same book
(VI, 742–746), is of particular interest in reference to this one,
because it affirms what is earlier brought into question: the poet's
ability to write poetry. If we read the poet's questions about
poetry in terms of the imagery of each passage, we find that the
incipient self-consciousness of the earlier passage—presented in
terms of the unfathered vapor—is in the later passage superseded
and resolved by the images of the kindred stream and the con-
federate gale. Again in Book XIII, referring to himself, Wordsworth speaks of

>   An insight that in some sort he possesses,
>   A privilege whereby a work of his,
>   Proceeding from a source of untaught things
>   Creative and enduring, may become
>   A power like one of Nature's.   [308–312]

Though it would be possible to see in this passage an element of
rivalry between poetry and nature, Wordsworth again restates the
basic unity of mind and nature by stressing that the origin of the
poetic act lies in a source of untaught things. The relationship is
intuitive, and intuited. Generating in a bond, it restates the existence of that bond. Consciously or unconsciously, Wordsworth's
imagination conceives of its relationship with nature in tauto-
logical terms:

>   For themselves create
> A like existence; and, whene'er it dawns
> Created for them, catch it, or are caught
> By its inevitable mastery.   [XIV, 94–97]

The poetic creation is here conceived as a "dawn," an epiphanic
manifestation of that which *is*, an expression of Being in the
world of becoming. In fact, it little matters whether the self
"catches" or "is caught" by this creation. As long as creation is
revelation of a power exterior to the self, or of one that exists both
in the outside world and in the self, thus binding inner and outer,
self-consciousness does not enter, and poetry is not problematic.
The creation dawns created, and the poetic self in the act of
creation "becomes" something larger than itself, passes into Being.
Poetry, again, is an act of integration for Wordsworth, a restate-
ment of the bonds between self and world. As long as catching
and being caught lead to the same result, no tension will exist between the creating self and the exterior world.

Yet Wordsworth is not unaware of the problematic elements in
poetry. He does at times conceive of the possibility of a self-
conscious creation and of poetry as an act of alienation, but
promptly rejects these. *The Prelude,* in fact, is an affirmation of
poetry's capacity to link the poet to the natural world. When he
does speak of self-consciousness, and of *ex-nihilo* creations, he is
usually referring to the Coleridgean imagination, far more a
product of the city and far more "liberated" from nature. On the
one hand Wordsworth will contend that poetry must loosen its
bonds with nature to become truly creative, truly imaginative,
and to lead to a revelation of the transcendent. On the other

hand, he will also contend that creation is an integration of self
and world, because it reveals the presence of the transcendent in
both man and nature. Without this concept of a transcendent and
all-encompassing reality, Wordsworth would most probably have
to choose between catching and being caught, between creating a
poetic world in nature's spite or drowning in the plenitude of
reality. Poetry in the nineteenth and twentieth centuries tends to
walk this narrow ridge between two abysses, often unsuccessfully.
Wordsworth, more successfully than most, balances these extremes. He does recognize, however, the danger inherent in their
pursuit:

> words for things,
> The self-created sustenance of a mind
> Debarred from Nature's living images,
> Compelled to be a life unto herself,
> And unrelentingly possessed by thirst
> Of greatness, love, and beauty.   [*The Prelude,* VI, 300–305]

Wordsworth describes specifically here the type of self-conscious
imagination he rejects, an imagination that creates a world out of
itself and must of necessity be at odds with nature. The images of
imprisonment leave no doubt as to the value judgment Wordsworth is making. The mind is "debarred," denied access to the
living world. It is locked within itself, trapped, "compelled" to
retain its integrity in opposition to its yearning. Nothing could be
farther from the "kindred stream" and the "correspondent
breeze." Mind and nature inhabit realms that are distinct, clear-
cut, and irreconcilable.

Ironically, Wordsworth does at times feel this enclosure and
debarment which he claims to bypass in *The Prelude*. These are
of course isolated instances, but they do point to the inability of
the romantic imagination to fully transcend or resolve its inner
dialectic. Sometimes, the balance between nature and imagination
is precarious, and the poet is on the verge of discovering that the
poetic imagination is indeed self-consciously creative, that it
"vexes itself *into* creation"[16] instead of being a power that "half-

16. Hartman, *The Unmediated Vision,* p. 12.

creates" and "half-perceives." The two ascension passages of *The Prelude* attempt to dissolve this inner tension of the imagination by contending that creation is revelation, placing it thus within the context of a larger, transcendent reality. Yet paradoxically the first ascension passage (VI, 592–640) will create most clearly in *The Prelude* the problem that it wishes to solve.

The Soulless Image

At the end of Book V of *The Prelude* Wordsworth repeats the statement of the "Intimations Ode": that the light seen at first in the natural world does not pertain to nature but to another realm. This notion is crucial to the ascension passages of *The Prelude,* because it gives the poet a basis for transcending nature without denying nature's importance or function. It allows him to claim that to ascend is not to withdraw from nature but to see it from the perspective of infinitude. A third perspective apparently is added here (as in the "Intimations Ode") to the natural and the temporal, possibly containing and resolving them. Yet this turn toward the infinite and the transcendent heightens instead the dialectic. The imagination that ascends the Alps tends to transcend both nature and time and in that sense to bring them together. But the ascension itself tends to permanently dissociate the imagination from nature and to turn it self-consciously creative.

The high point of the ascension of the poetic imagination occurs in Book VI of *The Prelude:*

> Imagination—here the Power so called
> Through sad incompetence of human speech,
> That awful Power rose from the mind's abyss
> Like an unfathered vapour that enwraps,
> At once, some lonely traveller. I was lost;
> Halted without an effort to break through. [592–597]

The imagination in this passage is rising gratuitously, not from phenomenal reality but from the mind's abyss: the imaginative power is rooted not in the natural world but in a consciousness that turns in upon itself. The unfathered quality of the vapor attests to this gratuitousness. Rising as an act of consciousness, without reason for being, the imagination enwraps the traveler in a realization of his own gratuity. Hovering between the phenomenal world of sensory perception and the intangible world of vision, the poet is "halted," "usurpcd" by his own interiority.

Yet the lines that follow place the experience in a different perspective and avoid a dissociation of the poetic imagination from the natural world:

> But to my conscious soul I now can say—
> 'I recognise thy glory:' in such strength
> Of usurpation, when the light of sense
> Goes out, but with a flash that has revealed
> The invisible world, doth greatness make abode,
> There harbours; whether we be young or old,
> Our destiny, our being's heart and home,
> Is with infinitude, and only there;
> With hope it is, hope that can never die,
> Effort, and expectation, and desire,
> And something evermore about to be.   [598–608]

Wordsworth quickly moves to make of this experience a connection rather than a disjunction between the phenomenal and the transcendent worlds. The mind which may well have recognized its autonomy from nature is instead usurped by a transcendent power—the Imagination itself. This perspective of an Imagination beyond the human, poetic imagination (Coleridge's primary imagination) usurps and binds the dialectical forces of nature and mind. The image of alienation and gratuitousness becomes, in this passage, one of integration and totality. The unfathered vapor emerges as independently from the human will as it does from nature. And as the light of sense goes out, the illumination hinted at in the "Intimations Ode" reappears to grant a continuity of vision between the phenomenal and the noumenal worlds. The creative, imaginative act is therefore not an *ex-nihilo* creation but an act of revelation and discovery. As with Coleridge's primary and secondary imagination, the creative imagination in Wordsworth draws away from the interiorization that accompanies a self-consciously creative mind and becomes a paradoxical link with the natural world from which it has withdrawn. By usurping the secondary imagination, the primary imagination has in one same movement transcendentalized it and redeemed it from gratuitousness and self-consciousness.

The second ascension passage, which occurs in Book XIV, overcomes the dialectic between the natural and the transcendent established momentarily in Book VI. The movement of ascension begins with a stagnant atmosphere—a "breezeless summer night, / Wan, dull, and glaring, with a dripping fog." As the travelers ascend, they are surrounded by mist. The initial difference between the two passages lies in the unequivocal origin of the mist in Book XIV. In Book VI there was a strong suggestion that the origin of the unfathered vapor was in the mind itself. The mist that envelops the travelers in Book XIV emerges from the natural world. The imminent fall into self-consciousness, which was suggested and bypassed in Book VI, is more successfully resolved in Book XIV. The poet achieves a vision of nature from the perspective of infinity. Yet the natural world is not transcended, but surrounded, usurped, by a power greater than itself. The poetic act which reveals this power is thus a means of relating both to nature and to the transcendent imagination, a force of discovery and revelation. The poet recognizes here that this power which is both natural and transcendent is ultimately the force that rolls through all things and endows nature with value.

Because Wordsworth can affirm this connection between the natural and the transcendent, he is able to descend, twice, from the Alps. Yet his descent is plagued by problems of perception, to the extent that it is not a true descent. The poet comes down from the "imaginative heights" (*The Excursion*, IV, 1188) to recover a world that had eluded him. Yet it is a world which he never truly recovers.

Even forms and substances are circumfused
By that transparent veil with light divine,
And, through the turnings intricate of verse,
Present themselves as objects recognised,
In flashes, and with glory not their own.

[*The Prelude*, V, 601–605]

Though these lines occur at the end of Book V, before the first ascension passage of *The Prelude*, we must assume that the poet, like Dante, or Hegel, or Saint Augustine, or any author engaged in confessional writing, is both protagonist and narrator, and to some extent possesses as narrator the knowledge not yet achieved by the protagonist. We began this section with a reference to this passage. The ascension passages of Books VI and XIV do not resolve but instead point back to the problems raised by it. Though the poet redescends into the natural world, he no longer recognizes objects in their immediacy but as potential vehicles for an experience of the transcendent. He no longer sees into them but through them, as if the objects were not really there, as if they were intimations of something "not their own." What these objects have lost, in the imagination's ascension and descent, is their ontological primacy. Once the imagination has ascended, there is no real return. Wordsworth descends, but he is no longer "there." He sees a universe in flux, partaking of an all-encompassing reality, but by the same token incapable of solidifying itself into recognizable shapes and forms. The real objects are gone. The light is no longer "their own." Again as in the "Intimations Ode" the transcendent light blinds the poet to the natural universe, and the veiling of objects with "light divine" becomes an enshrouding of them in opacity and darkness. The inward eye, the backward look, the movement of ascension achieve a continuity of vision only by a denial of what is most immediate in the natural world. To establish the continuity of response to nature sought after in "My heart leaps up" is precisely to lose the capacity to respond in such terms by the very methods used to regain it. In *Memorials of a Tour in Italy, 1837,* Wordsworth refers to the "baptized imagination" (XIV, 71). But the baptized imagination and the naturalized imagination are antithetical. The imagination baptized in "light divine" can intuit the transcendent; it can no longer see the real. The eye made quiet, in the last analysis, is the eye made blind.

In the context of this "failure" of the imagination to truly link these antithetical worlds, to truly redescend into reality, it is possible to consider another passage in Book VI—one of the most dense and contradictory in *The Prelude*, and which precedes the first ascension passage by some sixty lines—as a paradoxically simultaneous statement of the primacy of both the natural and the imaginative. The success of the balance between nature and imagination depends in this passage on the simultaneity of these opposing statements. To resolve it one way or the other, as we must, is to tautologically assume that such a balance does not exist.

> That very day,
> From a bare ridge we also first beheld
> Unveiled the summit of Mont Blanc, and grieved
> To have a soulless image on the eye
> That had usurped upon a living thought
> That never more could be.   [VI, 523–528]

The image of usurpation is perhaps central to the passage. In Book XIV the "solid vapours" usurp the majesty of the Atlantic. Later in Book VI the transcendent imagination usurps sensory perception. If we take, as Wordsworth does, the "soulless image" to be the object itself, and the "living thought" the imaginative intuition of the transcendent, the object would, by its closeness to the perceiver, usurp and undermine his capacity to transcend sensory perception into an intuition of the absolute. The poetic imagination moves in this passage away from the immediate and overwhelming presence of the object. If Mont Blanc is to be a symbol of transcendent power, it must not be so immediately unveiled. It must remain, as for Shelley, an "unsculptured image,"[17] or as for Wordsworth himself in Book VI, an "untransmuted

17. "Mont Blanc."

shape." Wordsworth grieves to have the summit so suddenly unveiled, without preparation, as he grieves to have crossed the Alps
without knowing, without endowing the act with a profound
ontological significance. The "soulless image on the eye" is thus
the sudden objective presence of Mont Blanc deprived of its
imaginative, ontological significance. The object, in this passage,
usurps the "living thought," the image that might have been and
never more can be.

We can see from an earlier passage in *The Prelude* (VI, 300–
305) that Wordsworth does not make a clear distinction between
the notions of image and natural object. If the image, that is, the
object, is "soulless," it is because some error has been committed
on the part of the perceiving self. But we can also see in this passage (VI, 523–528) the dangerous trajectory on which the poetic
imagination embarks when it is forced to deny the ontological
primacy of the object in order to affirm a transcendent reality.
The image of usurpation then moves in a different direction. We
may in fact, with some perverseness, take the soulless image to be
the poetic image itself, usurping and destroying, in its process of
ascension, the immediacy of the natural object. It is not the
sudden presence of Mont Blanc, but the soulless image in its
passage toward the abstract and the transcendent—Stevens calls
it a "spiritous passage into nothingness"[18]—that robs the object
of its ontological validity. The problem in reading these passages
in *The Prelude* is that Wordsworth maintains that the dialectic
operates between nature and poetry, nature and imagination,
whereas it may be seen working between the immediacy of the
object and the transcendence which precludes its immediate cognition. The contradictory possibilities of this passage are brought
out by the dual applicability of "that" in line 527. "That" refers
to both the soulless image of Mont Blanc and the eye of the poet
that "images" the object, transcending it in order to paradoxically
validate it. That the validation occurs with a vengeance and ends
in the desacralization of the object is also contained in the

18. "Of Heaven Considered as a Tomb."

ambivalence of "that." The poetic image, in this passage, is supposed to inform the object. When it does not, the eye of the poet, faced with the presence of nature, halts the progress of his song. Yet again, we may perversely suggest that it is the assertion of the poetic image in its opposition to the object which generates in this passage a simultaneous movement of inwardness and ascension that halts the progress of the poet's song. This is, as we have seen in the 1805 version, what in fact "halts" the traveler: not the perception of the object, but the vision of the imagination. The process of ascension makes this inwardness more acute, even though Wordsworth paradoxically ascends to withstall, or resolve, the movement of interiorization and withdrawal from nature. The image can only "in-form" the object by withdrawing from it (though by speaking of "nature's living images" Wordsworth deliberately confuses the image and its object). But in this movement away from the object the poetic image risks becoming soulless and disincarnated[19] and is finally confronted with the dark abyss of self-consciousness and interiorization from which it must pull back—from which it does pull back in Wordsworth—if poetry itself is to survive.

This dialectic operating between image and object, or imagination and natural reality, is thus profoundly paradoxical. The poetic image must refuse itself the conceptual ultimacy of the summits and seek the immediacy of the natural object. But in gravitating toward the natural object it must also preserve its interior distance and finally reject the longed-for plenitude in order to retain its integrity, in fact, remain itself.

The False Dawn

The disjunction between nature and imagination, the immediate and the transcendent, operates as well—as we have seen in the Lucy poems and "There was a Boy"—between the natural and the temporal, and between the protagonist's experience and the

---

19. The two terms may appear mutually exclusive, yet Wordsworth himself conceives of "soul" in terms of the self's relation to reality.

poet's creation. Through "emotions recollected in tranquillity" Wordsworth attempts to "re-collect" himself, to bring together two alien selves, what he was and what he is, in the deep vision of the "eye made quiet." But the notion of recollection introduces into the poetic structure a consciousness of temporality that precludes the experience the poet is trying to achieve.

The Wordsworthian act of recollection is indeed supposed to be an act of harvesting. In "A Poet's Epitaph" Wordsworth speaks of "the harvest of a quiet eye," implying that only the eye that is made quiet, stilled, denied the immediacy of perception, can effect a gathering of past and present into a more than existential unity. Ironically, the grave that appeared in "There was a Boy" as an irrevocable image of time in nature reappears in "A Poet's Epitaph" in relation to the quiet eye of recollection.

The act of poetry is for Wordsworth in the deepest sense an act of recollection. But it is an act which operates by a denial of the moment and the immediate perception of the eye, so that the poem affirms the very temporality it attempts to transcend and denies the virtual presence of the protagonist in the experience he is recounting. In "The Solitary Reaper" this dialectical relationship between the experience and the poetic creation stands out as the real theme of the poem. What we have first of all is a structure within a structure—a song contained in the poetic structure as a theme, but at the same time outside the poem's reach. A similar situation occurs in Stevens' "The Idea of Order at Key West." The girl there sings a song that cannot be translated into poetic language and must therefore remain on the other side of silence. Yet the song humanizes the poet's world, bringing order out of chaos without irrevocably transforming and destroying reality. It "sings" reality, without language, and thus stands at the threshold of the experience the poem retells. Stevens tends to create this kind of potential experience at the very center of his poems, so that the poem often fluctuates between silence and speech. In other words, we tend to feel that the girl's song may at any moment come into the world of the poem, or that the poem may indeed dissolve into the silent world of the song. Though the song must by definition stand outside the world of the poem, it tends in Stevens to be woven into the poetic structure, thrusting the poem into a potential presentness.

The song of the girl in "The Solitary Reaper" operates very differently. It does not give the impression of dissolving in the poem that contains it, rather it seems to stand off from the poem and make itself inaccessible to the protagonist who recounts the experience. The experience of the protagonist is his listening to the girl's song. But the encounter is clothed in an irrevocable pastness, and the content of the experience is sealed off from the poetic approach. Again, the problem of the relationship of song and poem refers to the relationship between the temporal and the natural, or the moment of experience and the temporal perspective. Wordsworth's attempt to make of poetry an act of recollection paradoxically casts the initial experience back into the past, and the poem never becomes the act of harvesting that the song is for the reaper. For the reaper, reaping and singing are simultaneous acts. There is no poetic act of creation to speak of in her song. Her utterance is as unselfconscious as the song of the nightingale later in the poem, and hence strictly "atemporal." We see the concepts of temporality, self-consciousness, artistic creation begin to cluster and oppose themselves to the natural and the unselfconscious. The boy of Winander must die in order to remain within the natural perspective. The solitary reaper must remain inaccessible to the world of the poem. Of course, we may contend that it is precisely as an inaccessible figure that she becomes intellectually accessible to us. Nevertheless, to say she is inaccessible is already to place her in an intellectual category. She is more than that. She is a figure on the borderline between silence and speech. She is the world the poet has lost and which he wishes to re-enter from this side of consciousness. She is also the danger which Wordsworth does not risk. Stevens will come far closer to poetic dissolution in the instant of experience, precisely because he validates the "irrational moment [in] its unreasoning."[20]

20. "Notes toward a Supreme Fiction ("It Must Give Pleasure," I).

Wordsworth will step back from the experience, and though the protagonist-poet is ostensibly in the presence of the reaper, the poetic act itself roots the experience in a temporal perspective in which its validity lies precisely in its pastness. Thus the poem that recollects the protagonist's experience of listening to the reaper denies itself access to the very world it recollects. The simultaneity of singing and reaping of the solitary figure is translated for the poet into a disjunction between the poetic act and the experience, between the temporal (mnemonic) structure of the poem and the momentary experience which is its theme.

We thus have in this apparently simple poem a very complex structure, built on the interrelationships of two past tenses—the past tense of the protagonist's encounter (revealed as such at the end of the poem) and the past tense of the poetic structure itself —and the virtual present of the song of the reaper, never actualized. The ontologically valid experience and its aesthetic representation operate for Wordsworth at two distinct levels which seldom if ever come together in his poems. Time and again he confronts an arresting situation, but unlike the protagonist of Müller's "Der Lindenbaum" he never feels the temptation to linger, and so his encounters are always with worlds from which he must "gently pass."

> Behold her, single in the field,
> Yon solitary Highland Lass!
> Reaping and singing by herself;
> Stop here, or gently pass!

The poet's exhortation suggests indeed that he has stopped, that the solitary figure in the natural world has arrested his attention and his passage (though the poem itself is proof that he has opted to pass). She is—like so many solitary figures in Wordsworth—somewhere between the human and the natural, going through human motions yet uttering sounds which though human remain foreign to the protagonist. Ultimately the most succinct description we have of her is "by herself," a human yet alien

figure, in the way nature remains alien to the human. Wordsworth sees in these solitary figures images of fusion of two dialectical worlds. Yet they also function as images of disjunction,
forcing the protagonist to recognize that these figures remain
closed within themselves, refusing to yield to him and to us the
secret of their presence. The vale overflows with the sound, but
the protagonist attempts to describe the song in terms that deliberately do not suffice: "No Nightingale did ever chaunt . . . ,"
"A voice so thrilling ne'er was heard / In spring-time from the
Cuckoo-bird." To say that the reaper's song is more than any of
these is to stop on this side of silence. Wordsworth's poems invariably do this. There is undoubtedly a dialectic operating between
poem and song, but the poem not only does not enter the world
it envisions, it consciously remains outside its confines. Rilke defines the poet (Orpheus) as he who oversteps (*überschreitet*) and
therefore risks annihilation. Wordsworth does not overstep the
boundaries of the given, and when, as in this poem, an extraor-
dinary experience has taken place, he approaches it from this
side of time and consciousness, where regardless of the apparent
drive toward the natural in the poem the distinctions remain
clearly drawn.

The third stanza raises questions about the content of the song.
"Will no one tell me what she sings?" The questions, rhetorical or
not, point once again to the inaccessibility of the world of the
song and underscore the distinction already established between
the natural and the temporal perspectives, the initial experience
and its aesthetic representation. The poem creates a kind of
center, a potential present and presence at the very heart of its
temporal structure. But the very presence of the song underlines
the perspective of time from which it is apprehended. "I saw her
singing at her work." This coupling of a past tense with a progressive tense is not uncommon in Wordsworth.[21] It indicates
here, as it does so many other times, that the significant experience for the poet takes place not within the natural but within

21. See *The Prelude*, I, 367–369; IV, 320–321; VII, 144.

the temporal realm, in spite of his attempt to synthesize them.
At the end of the poem, we find that encounters such as this between the temporal and the natural are not dissolved but preserved by being placed within the structure of time.

> What'er the theme, the Maiden sang
> As if her song could have no ending;
> I saw her singing at her work,
> And o'er the sickle bending:—
> I listened, motionless and still;
> And, as I mounted up the hill,
> The music in my heart I bore,
> Long after it was heard no more.

The girl's song neither ends nor begins, it is simply there, with a
forcefulness that makes the protagonist appear as an intruder.
The poet in the last stanza reasserts the eternal presentness of the
reaper's song—the act of singing which is forever an act of reaping, a spontaneous creation and remembering. Because of its
capacity to turn creation and recollection into reaping, the song
redeems in a sense its temporal finiteness; it becomes part of the
world that Lucy dead inhabits. The solitary reaper sings, and her
song is a harvesting of time in the natural world. It is the precise
though opposite equivalent of the grave in "There was a Boy."
The poet creates the poem and envisions a world of temporal-
natural synthesis from which he must "gently pass."

The ending of "To a Highland Girl" reasserts a similar perspective. The experience which has taken place (actually before
the narrative present) is allowed to pass into the temporal perspective with a reaffirmation of the poet's ability to recall the protagonist and the scenery and recollect his encounter:

> Joy have I had; and going hence
> I bear away my recompense. . . .
> For I, methinks, till I grow old,
> As fair before me shall behold,
> As I do now . . .

The problematic elements of memory in "Tintern Abbey" are

bypassed here with the simple assertion that memory can sustain and represent the poet's encounter.

"To a Painter," composed much later in 1840 and published in 1842, brings up more clearly than does "The Solitary Reaper" the limits of Wordsworthian recollections:

> All praise the Likeness by thy skill portrayed;
> But 'tis a fruitless task to paint for me,
> Who, yielding not to changes Time has made,
> By the habitual light of memory see
> Eyes unbedimmed, see bloom that cannot fade. . . .
> Couldst thou go back into far-distant years,
> Or share with me, fond thought! that inward eye,
> Then, and then only, Painter! could thy Art
> The visual powers of Nature satisfy.

Evidently between the poet's and the painter's vision stretch a number of years, years which have transformed the subject of the painting. The poet, however, is unyielding to the "changes Time has made" and sustains his initial vision of the unnamed protagonist by a refusal to accept what he accepts with so much grace in "Tintern Abbey"—the passage of time and the concomitant transformation of the self and the world the poet has known. Memory becomes in this poem not a transcendence of temporality—since temporality is introduced by the different visions of the same subject, by poet and painter, at different times—but a refusal to accept what the poet has no choice but to accept. And yet, a choice is there—perhaps unacceptable because so obviously wishful thinking, but a choice nevertheless. Wordsworth returns in this poem to the "inward eye" which appeared in "I wandered lonely as a cloud" as a rite of passage between past and present, an ability to recollect as well as embellish the initial experience. The wish that the painter could share the inward eye of the poet, thus transcending the irreversibility of the temporal perspective, is furthermore given in terms of (were it to happen) the artist's ability to "the visual powers of Nature satisfy." Nature is here associated with the prior vision that the poet had of the subject of the painting, and with the sustaining of that vision. Nature, in fact, is associated with the inward eye rather than the eye that perceives the visible, and thus with a timeless vision at the heart of the temporal perspective. Wordsworth is constant in his refusal to accept the abyss that so obviously exists in this poem between the temporal and the "natural," yet his refusal is given in the context of an impossible wish fulfillment, and becomes finally a reluctant acceptance of that abyss. The inward eye sustains a vision that is true to the poet's memory, true perhaps to "nature" as it was, but not authentic within the perspective of time.

What Wordsworth finally demands of his poetry—what is perhaps demanded of it—is not the breadth of vision that encompasses nature and time (since we have seen such a vision break down), but the containment of the poem's experience in a place where the tension between nature and time, nature and imagination, perception and vision, becomes unproblematic. Occasionally—though this is by no means a major or even a recurring theme in Wordsworth's poetry—we find such poems of enclosure. In the first of the *Miscellaneous Sonnets,* for instance, the poet affirms his capacity for happiness within the narrow confines of the sonnet's structure:

> Nuns fret not at their convent's narrow room;
> And hermits are contented with their cells;
> And students with their pensive citadels. . . .
> In truth the prison, unto which we doom
> Ourselves, no prison is: and hence for me,
> In sundry moods, 'twas pastime to be bound
> Within the Sonnet's scanty plot of ground.

The similes put forth here enable us to infer that what the poet is talking about is not so much the sonnet as it is the poetic vision itself. The images of enclosure associated with nuns, hermits, students, are images of contentment—maids, bees. And the prison thus conceived and validated becomes the significant space for the poetic experience.

The poet, however, does not remain with this imagery of enclosure. The confinement is there to provide "brief solace." Were it to lengthen its temporal existence, it would turn from solace to imprisonment and isolation.

This isolation becomes in "Captivity.—Mary Queen of Scots" (published in 1819) the subject of the poem:

> "As the cold aspect of a sunless way
> Strikes through the Traveller's frame with deadlier chill . . .
> So joys, remembered without wish or will,
> Sharpen the keenest edge of present ill,—
> On the crushed heart a heavier burthen lay.
> Just Heaven, contract the compass of my mind
> To fit proportion with my altered state!
> Quench those felicities whose light I find
> Reflected in my bosom all too late!—
> O be my spirit, like my thraldom, strait;
> And, like mine eyes that stream with sorrow, blind!"

The protagonist—both queen and poet—is a captive of the enclosed space, an enclosed space which is itself an image of memory. Nature is barren, cold, sunless, alien, and an "unparticipated ray" seems to underscore the protagonist's isolation from this sporadic intrusion of light. This unparticipated ray, we learn in the next few lines, is actually a memory of joy—a memory which functions, like the ray itself, as an underscoring of darkness and joylessness, but also as an image of rupture between past and present, a vision whose presence paradoxically proclaims its inaccessibility. The dimension of transcendence which allows the movement back into the past also allows this unwilled recollection in the midst of the captive's dispossession. The remembered experience, unlike that of "Tintern Abbey," the "Intimations Ode," and *The Prelude*, serves here to strengthen the poet's bonds to the temporal perspective and the space-in-time in which he finds himself enclosed. It serves, in fact, to unavoidably bring on the contraction which the protagonist demands. Mary Queen of Scots calls for the absence of memory as a relief from the oppressive unhappiness of the present. The poet equally demands the contraction of his vision—the vision that linked past and present in "Tintern Abbey"—to avoid the pain of "felicities" that are "reflected . . . all too late." We may of course argue that Wordsworth's choice of subject is not proof of his spiritual kinship with the protagonist's situation. But the all-too-late reflection of the past into the present does lead us back to the sad per-plexity of "Tintern Abbey" and to the systematic refusal of the poet to give up the more encompassing and in that sense more fulfilling temporal perspective—the after-meditations on experi-ences—for the present and presence of the experiences themselves. The "all too late" refers us back to Wordsworth's rejection of the moment—the moment that is a passage into the natural perspec-tive—for the perspective of time in which such moments are redeemed from their finiteness, but at the same time irrevocably lost.

Finally, the demand for blindness to the eyes bent on the in-ward vision points once again to the recognition of the sad perplexity, of a disjunction between what was and is, what was experienced and what was gleaned from the experience. The fruitfulness of the poetic act, its process of tranquil restoration sustained in "Tintern Abbey" and *The Prelude,* become in this poem a barren, enclosed space in which the remembrance of things past points only to their irretrievability. The demand for blindness seems here to be the final rejection of the inward eye, the eye made quiet of "Tintern Abbey," the eye of memory which saw into the past without ever transcending its pastness, going beyond its temporality. The inward eye, as we have seen, is simultaneous with the temporal perspective which memory affirms and in which it operates, and with the upward moment of the imagination which results, if not in the isolation of self-conscious-ness, certainly in the incapacity to relate to the particular and the immediate in the natural world. Just as Mary Queen of Scots demands that which she has no choice but to accept, the poet's call for blindness suggests that the blindness has been long con-tracted, and that in turn a blinding of the inward eye is required to obliterate the "unparticipated ray" which brings back so poignantly the memory of vision and its loss. Seeking the tran-scendent and unifying light, the Wordsworthian imagination is made captive by a transcending and temporalizing (and in that sense blinding) movement away from immediate perception. The memory of vision in fact points far more to its absence (that is, its temporal ficticity) than to its presence. The light occasionally comes, but like Bonnefoy's "aube d'un second jour," which appears only to give way to "le jour gris,"[22] Wordsworth's "welcome light"

> Dawns from the east, but dawns to disappear
> And mock [him] with a sky that ripens not
> Into a steady morning. [*The Prelude*, I, 125–127]

The attempted resolution of the dialectic between nature and imagination, nature and time, leads into a profounder discontinuity. And the captive of this abstractive imagination, who sought to transcend and contain these antithetical modes of being, blinds himself watching for the light that does not dawn.

22. Yves Bonnefoy, *Hier régnant désert* (Paris: Mercure de France, 1958). "Le Visage mortel," pp. 34, 27.

⚞ YEATS

In *A Vision* Yeats speaks of an early Byzantine period in which there was a unified perspective on reality, and in which the artist, creating out of that unity, brought forth a vision of things that was shared by all.

I think that in early Byzantium, maybe never before or since in recorded history, religious, aesthetic and practical life were one, that architect and artificers—though not, it may be, poets, for language had been the instrument of controversy and must have grown abstract—spoke to the multitude and the few alike. The painter, the mosaic worker, the worker in gold and silver, the illuminator of sacred books, were almost impersonal, almost perhaps without the consciousness of individual design, absorbed in their subject-matter and that the vision of a whole people.[1]

This oneness between the artist and the exterior world, the artist and his community, made of him less an artist than an artisan, creating not in an act of consciousness in its isolation from reality but in an act of reality itself. The history of art, as Malraux points out,[2] is a trajectory from the perspective of reality to that of consciousness, from anonymity to the self-portrait. Even when

1. W. B. Yeats, *A Vision*, a reissue with the author's final revisions (New York: Macmillan, 1956), pp. 279–280.

2. See especially *Les Voix du silence* (Paris: Pléiade, 1951), and *La Psychologie de l'art*, Vol. II: "La Création artistique" (Genève: Skira, 1947), p. 212.

the self is not so obviously depicted, the artist is "imperiously present"[3] in his work, and whatever his subject, he portrays not the world, but himself. Instead of the impersonality and anonymity of Byzantine art (to some extent medieval art as well), the modern world witnesses the phenomenon of an art so conscious of itself that it no longer attempts to be representational.

In *The Voices of Silence* Malraux discusses briefly a Sung "style" of painting of the thirteenth century:[4] an enormous lake, a huge mountain, a metaphysical fog; in the middle of the lake, a small boat with three infinitesimally small human figures. The human is here absorbed by the natural, engulfed by infinitude, and no tension seems to exist. The human in Western art, on the other hand, seems to be constantly at odds with the natural, and to resolve the tension between them is to reduce this paradoxical and disturbing art to silence.

Yet artists do try to resolve the dialectic, and what emerges out of this attempt is a literature of extremes, a poetry at the very limits of language. To resolve this tension between the human and the natural, the poet will either risk drowning in reality or create an intentional universe "in nature's spite" (*CP*, 238), one which denies the existence of what Wordsworth terms "existing things." Wordsworth rejects the "powerless trance" of the natural for the "inevitable mastery" of the transcendent. (In the Sung painting referred to above the natural and the infinite are part of a single conception.) Yet he keeps a balance between imagination and reality which prevents him from falling into either abyss. Yeats goes much further in the direction of the imaginative and the intentional, attempting to construct a world in which, as in the early historical Byzantium, the artist can be totally himself and the world.

Yeats's poetry, like Wordsworth's, thus stems from a profound sense of loss of the unity of being. But where Wordsworth defines loss in terms of the self's relationship to nature, Yeats couches it, at least initially, in mythological terms. "The woods of Arcady

3. Malraux, *La Psychologie de l'art*, II, 212.
4. Malraux, *Les Voix du silence*, p. 331.

are dead, / And over is their antique joy" (*CP*, 7). Yeats's attachment to the early Byzantine period bespeaks his fascination with man's ability to live in myth, at one with himself and with the exterior world. What is lost in the modern world is precisely the mythological dimension which allowed him to participate in the life around him, to see himself as part of a larger whole. "Seeing into myth," says Ammons, "is / knowledge myth can't sanctify."[5] Once this dimension is broken, man is thrown back upon himself, an outcast in an unintelligible world. The knowledge of myth stems from the destruction of the unity of being and in turn bars the self from regaining that unity. The human consciousness which in Wordsworth divorces the child from nature and makes him pass into the temporal perspective forces the self in Yeats to pass into "the desolation of reality" (*CP*, 287), a place of dispossession where both self and world are only what Stevens calls "fragments found in the grass."[6]

We find in Yeats the same attempt to re-enter that realm of being from this side of history—to regain, through consciousness, what is lost by an act of consciousness itself. Like the early Stevens, but without the sense of impossibility that Stevens brings to his attempts at creating worlds, Yeats begins to construct a world in which the self can be complete, totally itself and its world. He never becomes, of course, the artificer of Irish history, never creates the valid myth. (Indeed, the very notion of creating myth is antithetical to the Western idea of myth itself.) But he does attempt to construct a world where the imagination transcends both nature and time and where the self grasps itself as subject and object of its genesis.

The world Yeats constructs is thus at the very outset doomed by the self-consciousness with which it is created. It is a world constructed "in nature's spite," and ultimately inimical to the very idea of poetic creation. Wordsworth sought the unity of being first in the self's relation to the natural, then in its relation to the transcendent. Both were intemporal worlds, antithetical to

5. A. R. Ammons, "Crevice."
6. "Two Illustrations That the World Is What You Make of It."

the temporal perspective from within which the poet created. For Yeats the distinction between the temporal and the natural does not exist. Both nature and time point to the limitation of the self, and both have to be transcended for the poet to arrive at the intentional creation in which he can be both consciousness and reality, the creating self and the created world.[7]

But this attempted wholeness of the self results in a clear distinction between narrator and protagonist, the creator of the poem and the fictional self within the poem. Out of nature and out of time, the self is a fictive self, intentionally created but by the same token unable to create, unable to give, as Stevens will say, "of bird or bush."[8] Nature and time, inimical as they are to the completeness Yeats is seeking, are also the only realms in which the poet can validly create. Yeats discovers, as Stevens will, that the intentional creation, created in opposition to the temporal and the natural perspectives, locks him in a world where the knowledge necessary for completeness becomes deathlike and deadening. The quest for knowledge thus turns into a yearning for ignorance, and the affirmation that "words alone are certain good" (CP, 7) leads to a wish to throw "poor words away / And [be] content to live" (CP, 89). Yeats discovers, as Stevens will, that the quest for totality is inimical to the world of the living and to the act of poetry itself. The desolation of reality lies not so much in reality as in the act of poetry that creates in opposition to reality. And thus we see in the later Yeats a return to the temporal (natural) perspective, a recognition of the poet's capacity to find in history the occasion for tragic joy. The barren landscape becomes the place of exultation. And the affirmation of temporality leads paradoxically to the experience of being.

This affirmation of nature and time also transforms the poet's perspective on poetry. Yeats passes from the enclosed, self-contained world of "Sailing to Byzantium" to the historical world of

7. This antithesis between nature and time in Wordsworth and their simultaneity in Yeats is not surprising if we consider Yeats to be within Blake's mythical, apocalyptic tradition.
8. "Anecdote of the Jar."

"Lapis Lazuli," in which the artistic construct is deliberately vulnerable to the temporal perspective, and in fact is validated by the very temporality which erodes it. The lapis and the poem are simultaneously humanized and naturalized by time (the ravages of time on the lapis appear as natural avalanches), brought back into the world of the becoming, where being is neither real nor illusory, but only a mythical possibility.

Great Broken Rings

The death of the woods of Arcady and the loss of their antique joy spell man's fall from myth. But the fall from myth is a fall into the temporal perspective, where the self, a "dying animal" locked in time and dispossessed of the animal's wholeness, is doubly conscious of its incomplete identity. The poet begins, like Wordsworth, by looking at the past and recognizing his loss:

> 'What change has put my thoughts astray
> And eyes that had so keen a sight?
> What has turned to smoking wick
> Nature's pure unchanging light?'

This passage from "Tom the Lunatic" is rather unusual, because Yeats will not often place such value on the natural. Its importance, however, lies in the implicit confrontation between two temporally distinct selves. Sensory perception is affected by time, and through that change the natural is radically transformed. Wordsworth gracefully accepts change and loss by placing them within the perspective of growth. Yeats rebels against the ravages with which time afflicts the self.

Speaking without the aid of a "mad" protagonist, Yeats raises a similar problem in "Towards Break of Day":

> My memories had magnified
> So many times childish delight.
>
> I would have touched it like a child
> But knew my finger could but have touched
> Cold stone and water.

Wordsworth conceives of the changes evidenced by memory as part of a process of maturation. Yeats's world is infinitely less reassuring. He is conscious not only of the irretrievability of what he remembers, but also of the "magnification" of the content of such memories, which casts doubt on their veracity and their validity. Memory is not a valid antidote to time in Yeats's universe. Stevens rejects memory because it reaffirms the temporal perspective and impedes any intimacy between self and world. Yeats rejects it because even if the act of memory did not transform the content of memory, the mature man's sensory perception would be incapable of retrieving the child's experience of things.[9] The waterfall he speaks about earlier in the poem is no longer a waterfall but "cold stone and water," beyond the reach of the temporal self. "Man is in love and loves what vanishes, / What more is there to say?" (*CP*, 205). The self in Yeats is constantly assailed by time, loving what vanishes and seeing itself destroyed, and this acute consciousness of time as a process of disintegration will lead the poet to seek what does not vanish and, in fact, to create it.

This keen perception of the finiteness of things gives "The Wild Swans at Coole" its poignant beauty. The poem is, in a sense, Yeats's "Tintern Abbey," though without the ultimate resolution and affirmation that Wordsworth brings to his poem:

> The trees are in their autumn beauty,
> The woodland paths are dry,
> Under the October twilight the water
> Mirrors a still sky;
> Upon the brimming water among the stones
> Are nine-and-fifty swans.

The peacefulness and fulfillment in the natural scene of the first stanza underscore the tension felt by the poet within the temporal perspective. The stillness and fruition of autumn provide the occasion for the poet's wearied look at the lack of stillness and fruition in his life. Yet the anger against time which comes through in other poems is muted here into a quiet resignation.

9. Robert Frost deals with the same problem in "To Earthward."

Returning to the same scene nineteen years after, Yeats finds that all is changed. The swans are "unwearied still," but the assertion of continuity within the natural perspective serves to underline, as in "Tintern Abbey," the discontinuity of the self in time. The description of the swans points to the opposite though unuttered description of the poet: *"Their* hearts have not grown old; / Passion or conquest . . . / Attend upon them still" (my italics). The stillness of the autumn landscape is repeated adverbially and projected into a temporal landscape, suggesting recurrence and continuity. The connection between the temporal and the natural in "Tintern Abbey" pointed to a pattern of quiet restoration. The stillness which unites both realms here serves to distinguish the temporal self from the natural perspective in which such unity exists. The still sky of the opening stanza is mirrored by the still water of the last. But the poet mirroring himself in time against a previous encounter discovers that for him there is no stillness, temporally or naturally, in the fullest meaning of the term. The swans, still there, unwearied still, seem untouched by, impervious to the temporal world. But the poet perceives their movements in "great broken rings." Recurrence and continuity—captured in the double meaning of "still"—refer to a world no longer there. The poet's encounter forces him to recognize, simultaneously, the pastness of the past and the impossibility of the present encounter in the future. There is no "life and food / For future years" here. In Stevens' "Description without Place" "swans far off [are] swans to come," the apocalyptic vision spanning past and future in a placeless and timeless perspective. But the future in Yeats's poem holds only the expectation of swans that have flown away:

> But now they drift on the still water,
> Mysterious, beautiful;
> Among what rushes will they build,
> By what lake's edge or pool
> Delight men's eyes when I awake some day
> To find they have flown away?

The last stanza does not destroy the stillness and the continued presence of the swans, but it does project the poet from the dis-

tance of his present encounter to a further distance in time. The
magic stillness of the autumn landscape is not broken. But the
poet, unable to be fully drawn into the natural enchantment, finds
himself moving in "great broken rings." Like Wordsworth in
"Tintern Abbey," Yeats begins by telling time in terms of seasons
("The nineteenth autumn has come upon me") but ends by seeing
the seasons projected into an abstract, temporal world. There is
no Dorothy in this poem to contain the temporalization of the
natural. The faint presence of Maud Gonne[10] in fact accentuates
the estrangement of the poet's encounter. He "counts" the seasons
as he counts the swans, and the counting is in a strange sense already the "awakening" of the last stanza, the inability to move
within the wheeling rings of the swans.

Like "Tintern Abbey," "The Wild Swans at Coole" is an attempt to come to terms with loss. Occasionally, Yeats refuses to
do so, and in the guise of a mad or at least an eccentric protagonist he rebels against the inevitability of change: "I spit into the
face of Time / That has transfigured me" (CP, 46). Memory
here functions quite differently than in "The Wild Swans at
Coole." It becomes a mode of transcendence, a refutation of the
temporal perspective within which it exists. There is in this poem
("The Lamentation of the Old Pensioner") an acknowledgment
of change and, simultaneously, a refusal to consider its finality.
Memory, abstractive and transcendent, redeems the self from the
negative transfiguration it is faced with.

What is interesting about the function of memory in Yeats is
that it does not project him, as Wordsworth would wish, into the
natural world, but on the contrary seems to institute a movement
toward a changeless, timeless world. In "A Man Young and Old,"
X, the poet associates isolation with the peacock's cry, the peacock's cry with memory, memory with what is natural, what is
natural with a stone, and the stone with isolation: "Being all
alone I'd nurse a stone / And sing it lullaby" (CP, 223). What
is natural is what is intentional, or at least intemporal. Yeats fol-

10. See Bloom, Yeats, p. 191.

lows the implications of this logic without the reluctance that we find in Wordsworth. The affirmation of memory as a category of transcendence ends with a celebration of a changeless, impenetrable, and dead world. The stone retains, like the self, its "in-itselfness" and its isolation. And, unlike the self, it endures the erosion of time, untouched by either lullaby or peacock's cry. The most horrifying and strident sound, as well as the softest and gentlest, is incapable of breaking through that solidity. Yeats senses that this timeless world is inimical to life as well as creativity, that the self singing a lullaby to a stone may well become "en-chanted to a stone / To trouble the living stream" (*CP*, 179). The stone in "Easter 1916" does not seem to be part of the natural scene but stands in opposition to it, a symbol of a deaden-ing enchantment that does not partake of the changing seasons and "troubles" the living stream.

Yeats's use of the stone is at best ambiguous, however. For he sees in it both the transcendence of a temporality that consumes him and the deadening effect of such transcendence. The image of the stone is thus associated with the quest for the wholeness of self, and the rejection of that wholeness; with the quest for the timeless self, and the reaffirmation of temporality. Yeats is "look-ing for the face [he] had / Before the world was made" (*CP*, 266), but in his search for wholeness through self-knowledge rather than self-abandonment he discovers, as Wordsworth and Stevens do, that such knowledge is indeed purchased by the loss of power, and that the price of totality is an intemporal and fictive self. In "Ego Dominus Tuus" the self and the other discuss the value of the image through which such wholeness may be achieved. The tendency of the poem is to give weight to Ille's assertion that the anti-self by opposition and antithesis creates the occasion for this sought-for wholeness. Yet Hic's arguments, deliberately less philosophical and less cogent, point in the direction of Yeats's later thinking. Ille calls for his opposite "by the help of an image" and sees in the "image that might have been a stony face" of the opposite the possibility of completion. Hic does not have the last word in the poem, but he calls Ille's

efforts at wholeness "the unconquerable delusion" and sees an
irreconcilable conflict between the self and the image of the self:
"And I would find myself and not an image." The anti-self is
seen here as antithetical but not complementary to the self, in the
way that the image in the mirror in other poems appears as a
denial of wholeness rather than a pathway to it. Hic's vision of
art, predictably, is one in which art does not stem from an
achieved and deliberate completion but from a "deliberate happiness," from a oneness of self and world which is both necessary
and inimical to poetry: "Impulsive men that look for happiness /
And sing when they have found it." Hic is perhaps on the right
track, but without an understanding of the complexities of his
affirmation, his affirmation is invalidated. His assertion of the
necessity of oneness between self and world will be paralleled by
Yeats's assertion in the later poems that the poet must be involved
with time and history. But Yeats will have arrived at that assertion by an eccentric road that takes him first through Ille's thinking. The straightforward, uncomplicated affirmation put forth
by Hic sounds finally like the imitative art of those without imagination and points once again to the need for wholeness and
artistic "redemption."

Wholeness is conceived, in "A Prayer for My Daughter," in
terms of a soul which is both self and anti-self, the subject and
the object of its actions. In the conversational style of Coleridge's
"Frost at Midnight," but with darker overtones, Yeats speaks of
a search for innocence that stems from the knowledge of complexity, a search that begins in intricacy and leads to simplicity,
that begins in history and leads back into the garden. In "Frost at
Midnight" the "idling Spirit" is an "echo or mirror seeking of
itself," and the "secret ministry of frost" ends finally in the recovery of oneness that Yeats seeks. Coleridge projects, for his
child, a relationship between self and world which affirms the
wholeness of the self, a wholeness defined in natural terms by the
"silent icicles / Quietly shining to the quiet Moon." Adverb and
adjective, referring to different objects, bring these objects together, and the action of shining suggests a further relationship in

terms of image and reflection. The "echo or mirror seeking of
itself" of the beginning of the poem finds its response in the last
line, where the soul, beholding the object, discovers in the act of
perception that it is itself the mirror and the object mirrored—
the idling spirit, and the natural world. In a sense, this discovery
in "Frost at Midnight" is Hic's implicit but inarticulate wish in
"Ego Dominus Tuus."

There are, of course, major differences between "Frost at
Midnight" and "A Prayer for My Daughter." In Coleridge's poem
nature is hushed, and silently, unhelped by any wind, the frost
performs its secret ministry, which is the act of binding both the
child's and the poet's days, as Wordsworth wished, in "natural
piety." Coleridge looks to his past and, with a great deal more
security than Yeats can feel, thinks of his child's future. In Yeats's
poem, the howling storm and the screaming sea-wind find their
counterpart in the "great gloom" of the poet's mind. Instead of
the quiet ministry of frost, he finds in his vision of the future the
years "dancing to a frenzied drum, / Out of the murderous innocence of the sea." The "radical innocence" of the ninth stanza
is perhaps qualified in advance by the "murderous innocence" of
the second, so that Yeats's notion of innocence takes on, as Bloom
suggests,[11] the aspects of Blake's higher, organized innocence.

> The soul recovers radical innocence
> And learns at last that it is self-delighting,
> Self-appeasing, self-affrighting,
> And that its own sweet will is Heaven's will.

Innocence is associated in "Frost at Midnight" with the child's
ability to recognize in the silence of nature the eternal language
of an omnipresent God. It is not clear in Yeats's poem whether the
same recognition is posited, or whether the self bends Heaven's
will to its own, achieving wholeness by the containment of self
and world. The hush and quietness of nature in "Frost at Midnight" and the howling storm of "A Prayer for My Daughter"
frame perhaps two equally different perspectives on the nature of
innocence. Where Coleridge views innocence, as Wordsworth

11. *Yeats*, p. 326.

would, in terms of a quiet, almost self-effacing relationship with nature (at least in this poem), Yeats again sees in innocence not the initial but the final step in the self's quest for totality—an innocence, negatively posited in "Ego Dominus Tuus," which does not suggest simplicity but which contains and resolves the complexities of the historical perspective. Custom and ceremony, in the last stanza of "A Prayer for My Daughter," are wrought precisely out of this encounter with historical complexity, and in turn give birth to this innocence which transcends them.

Yet "A Prayer for My Daughter," like Ille in "Ego Dominus Tuus," raises a problem which Yeats does not fully articulate and which does not become fully evident until the poems that deal specifically with the poet's act of creation. The self which mirrors itself instead of nature, which finds totality by an unwilled yet inevitable retrenchment, tends to fall into a solipsistic world. Ille in "Ego Dominus Tuus," like the Soul in "A Dialogue of Self and Soul," seeks a completed image of the self which must be purchased at the cost of the living world. The image which Ille sees fashioned from its opposite is "an image that might have been a stony face," complete within itself, denying in fact the meaning of the image, which is that of reflection; but by that very completeness dead, impervious to the exterior world. The problem with the argument put forth by Ille, and by the Soul in "A Dialogue of Self and Soul," is that the exterior world is nonexistent, contained in the inwardness of the soul. The affirmation of completeness is based on the assumption that inwardness and exteriority are not dialectical forces, that one assumes and contains the other by the sheer affirmation that it does so. But fortunately for Yeats, as for Stevens, "the world stays," intruding persistently upon that inwardness, until it finally forces the poet to move outward once again into reality. The ascent of the soul into a higher innocence is not so much ascent as enclosure, not so much completion as rejection of what makes it incomplete. The dialectical forces of consciousness and reality are not synthesized by this movement but simply pulled apart in a way that denies the existence of the dialectic. Wordsworth comes down from the Alps and attempts to bind the autonomous imagination to natural reality. Stevens moves out of his enclosed world, into a world that has not been intentionally constructed. Yeats finds, already in "Ego Dominus Tuus," and more cogently in the "Dialogue," that the dialogue turns into a monologue only at the price of reality, that the Soul achieves completion but simultaneously becomes deaf and dumb and blind—its tongue a stone. In a paradoxical simultaneity of muteness and speech Wordsworth writes a poem— "There was a Boy"—about the self's inability to regain its pastness and thus achieve completion. It is perhaps the Self's affirmation of exteriority in Yeats's poem that retains the dialectic, sustaining thus the poetic act itself.

The Soul's argument involves a "steep ascent" which transcends history and nature and leads to the annihilation of the thought that generates it. This sounds a little like the mystical wholeness sought by the Soul. Yet it is a wholeness too easily affirmed, not achieved through the poem but asserted initially as a viable possibility. The Self affirms, in contrast, the historical perspective, though it too is a flawed perspective, a looking glass which reflects the past but a past locked in a changeless pattern, "unspotted by the centuries." Self and Soul are caught in this poem in the inner logic of their separate visions, and neither is capable of transcending its isolated perspective to arrive at the dialogue suggested in the title.

Perhaps the "Dialogue," which proceeds, as Bloom points out, as two separate monologues,[12] is indicative of Yeats's ambivalence toward the efforts of Self and Soul and of his inability to synthesize them. Yeats finds that he wishes both to affirm and to deny the temporal perspective that consumes him. He conceives of self-fulfillment, on the one hand, as a transcendence of the temporal and an acquisition of knowledge that is both knowledge of the self and of the world: "All could be known or shown / If Time were but gone" (*CP*, 253). Yet knowledge is not only problematic but dangerous, inimical to the world of experience. The Soul wishes to grow into itself, to become what it is, and instead

12. *Yeats,* pp. 373–374.

"grow[s] nothing, knowing all" (*CP*, 33). Yeats is cursed by the mutual exclusivity of knowledge and being, which finds its most explicit expression in the two trees of Eden and which no apocalyptic vision can synthesize. It is this recognition of the impossibility of arriving at the absolute self through knowledge and containment which leads him to affirm, sporadically, the value of ignorance and self-abandonment: "All knowledge lost in trance / Of sweeter ignorance" (*CP*, 143).[13]

The importance of "A Dialogue of Self and Soul" lies in the importance Yeats assigns to the imagination in the dialogue. To side with either perspective would be in a sense detrimental to the creative powers of the poet, if not inimical to creation. Yet the imagination is clearly associated with the vision of totality which the Soul pursues—unless of course such a relationship is merely the Soul's assumption and not poetic fact. The second speech of the Soul suggests that ontological primacy lies not in the temporal perspective, but in the imagination's rejection of the immediate and finite for the abstract and the unchanging:

> Think of ancestral night that can,
> If but imagination scorn the earth
> And intellect its wandering
> To this and that and t'other thing,
> Deliver from the crime of death and birth.

In Book XIII of *The Prelude* Wordsworth rejects "the mind intoxicate / With present objects, and the busy dance / Of things that pass away" for the "temperate show / Of objects that endure" (29–32). Yeats too rejects the temporal for the eternal, the finite for the abstract and the complete. The quest for the unified self is thus associated, as it was for Wordsworth, with a movement of ascension, a rejection of the natural for the intemporal and the enduring. The crime of death and birth occurs within the finiteness of the temporal. To be redeemed from it, the imagination must "scorn the earth" and by a movement inward discover within itself the cause of its own genesis. Hence the

13. See also "The Dawn": "I would be—for no knowledge is worth a straw— / Ignorant and wanton as the dawn."

necessity to move beyond the past, into the ancestral night in which the Soul discovers its origins, its "ancestry," in itself. "Who can distinguish darkness from the soul?" This darkness which Yeats associates with the soul is not very different from the too potent light which in Wordsworth blinds the poet to the specificity of the natural landscape. And the effects are equally detrimental. Wordsworth does not see in this movement upward and inward a fall into self-consciousness, but the danger of solipsism is clear in this and other Yeats poems. Perhaps this all too evident danger validates, in spite of its shortcomings, the historical perspective which the Self continues to affirm. In its second speech, the Self sustains the temporality within which it exists and the "charter to commit the crime once more," to inhabit reality and share in the finiteness of things.

The final speech of the Soul returns to the themes it established in its previous speeches, once again affirming its wholeness not as a possibility but as a fact: "Intellect no longer knows / *Is* from the *Ought,* or *Knower* from the *Known.*" In its achieved completeness, what is is prescriptive of what should be, and the self is both knower and known, a synthesis of consciousness and reality. Saint Paul in his first epistle to the Corinthians speaks of arriving at a heavenly stage in which he will know as he is known, in which inwardness and exteriority will coincide. In such coincidence the self becomes both subject and object of its knowledge, grasps itself in its totality, and transcends the Cartesian dialectic. Yet the final speech of the Soul contains much darker overtones:

> Such fullness in that quarter overflows
> And falls into the basin of the mind
> That man is stricken deaf and dumb and blind,
> For intellect no longer knows
> *Is* from the *Ought,* or *Knower* from the *Known*—
> That is to say, ascends to Heaven;
> Only the dead can be forgiven;
> But when I think of that my tongue's a stone.

The dialectic is transcended, again as in "Ego Dominus Tuus" and "A Prayer for My Daughter," by the annihilation of one of its poles, but total objectivity, or total subjectivity, ends in the reduction of the self to the "in-itselfness" of the object. The image of the stone returns in this poem to suggest that wholeness is antithetical to the conditions necessary to poetic creation. "I wish that I might be a thinking stone" says Stevens,[14] but no such thing exists in Yeats's or Stevens' world. The act of self-knowledge, conceived in its ultimate and extreme possibilities, is a reductive, not an integrative act. And its achieved completeness is that of the insentient object, which *is* but cannot know itself as *being*. "Only the dead can be forgiven" the gratuitousness of existence and temporality, but the price of such redemption is poetic silence and precisely death-in-life. In "Ode to a Nightingale" Keats recognizes the danger of following the natural object into the depths of the forest and losing the consciousness and isolation that make the poem possible. We find implicit in Yeats's "Dialogue" the opposite danger—not of drowning into plenitude, but of solidifying the self into an unnatural and deathlike wholeness. Poetry walks, gingerly at times, between these two abysses, knowing that to overstep in either direction is to reduce itself to stone.

What we have thus in this poem is a dialogue beneath the dialogue, a discussion not so much about wholeness versus finiteness, or essential simplicity versus existential complexity, but about the imagination's capacity for poetic speech. The problem that emerges in the major poems dealing with artistic creation is also raised here in reference to these two antithetical visions of intemporal wholeness and of finiteness and immediacy. Perhaps there is more danger in the Soul's attempt at wholeness than in the Self's validation of the temporal and the historical, and for that reason if no other the Self's final speech, which takes up the second part of the poem, seems to carry more weight. Indeed, it points to some extent in the direction in which Yeats's imagination will finally move. The Self affirms here the lack of knowledge (Yeats of course more than once validates ignorance), the

14. "Le Monocle de Mon Oncle."

gratuitousness of existence ("I am content to live it all again"),
and in choosing the temporal over the eternal it achieves a sudden
vision of reality:

> I am content to follow to its source
> Every event in action or in thought;
> Measure the lot; forgive myself the lot!
> When such as I cast out remorse
> So great a sweetness flows into the breast
> We must laugh and we must sing,
> We are blest by everything,
> Everything we look upon is blest.

The Self refers to and rejects the Soul's contention that only the
dead can be forgiven. It forgives itself "the lot," and in doing so
moves to an acceptance of the moment in its immediacy and to
an experience of eternity within the perspective of time.

   This validation of the moment occurs repeatedly in Yeats's
poetry. The Irish airman who foresees his death is led, by "a
lonely impulse of delight" (*CP*, 133), to seek intensity in the
moment that denies and annihilates all other moments. More
positively in "Stream and Sun at Glendalough," a motion of the
sun or stream pierces the poet's body through and regenerates
him, making him live "like these that seem / Self-born, born
anew." This is not the radical innocence of "A Prayer for My
Daughter," where the poet sought wholeness within the self.
Wholeness is achieved here in a momentary movement outward—
not a possession of time and the world, but a dissolving in the
moment of reality. Ultimately Yeats, like most poets, cannot transcend or synthesize the dialectic of possession and participation.
The self is reborn in this poem no longer out of an impulse within
itself but from its contact with exterior things, the contact that in
"Vacillation" allows the poet to feel that he is "blessèd and [can]
bless." What is interesting about the passage from "Stream and
Sun at Glendalough" is that, as will be the case in "Lapis Lazuli,"
the regeneration of the human is conceived in terms of its ability
to establish contact with the temporal. Similarly in "Her Triumph"
the chain is broken, and the poet stares "astonished at the sea, /

And a miraculous strange bird shrieks at us." The poet ("Saint George or else a pagan Perseus") destroys the monster that turns the self into stone, and makes possible a sudden momentary vision of the immediacy of things. The totality of the stone, affirmed in "Dialogue," "Prayer," and "Ego Dominus Tuus" as a symbol of the complete self, is transcended here in an affirmation of a completeness based not on intemporality, but on instantaneity; not on the isolated self, but on the self thrust into the immediacy of the natural world. The astonishment accompanies the seeing into things for the first time, the passage into being. In "The Phases of the Moon" the poet laughs "to think that what seemed hard / Should be so simple" as he watches a bat rise from the hazels and circle around him. The intentional world the self creates for itself is denied and transcended here, and once again the surprising perception of reality is coupled with a denial of the validity of the constructed world. The intemporal creation, as well as the intemporal and complete self, is bypassed for the instantaneous movement outward into the real, the sudden revelation. Once again, the temporal and the natural are conceived in Yeats's poetry in synthetical terms, and the dialectic which operates between the transcendent and the temporal, the vision of wholeness and the immediacy of things, creates the framework for poetic silence or poetic speech. The vision of totality, purchased by a total objectivity, entails the destruction of that which gives birth to the imagination itself. Mallarmé writes to Cazalis, "Happily I am completely dead."[15] The death of the personal, the historical, the subjective, is the prerequisite for the totality sought by the soul. Yet only within this more limited perspective, and out of the tension, indeed the dialectic, between the quest for wholeness and the recognition of its inaccessibility, the desire for order and the necessity for complexity, can the poetic imagination survive and validate itself. The dialogue between Self and Soul fails as a

15. "Heureusement, je suis parfaitement mort," Stéphane Mallarmé, *Correspondance,* ed. Henri Mondor (Paris: Gallimard, 1959), May 1867, I, 240.

dialogue. But it creates the occasion for this more subtle dialogue which the imagination carries on with itself. Self and Soul seem to feel the necessity to choose extreme positions. The Yeatsian imagination will be the synthesis which is absent (or only virtually present) in this poem, moving from the quest for changelessness of "Sailing to Byzantium" to the reaffirmation of the temporal perspective in "Lapis Lazuli."

In Nature's Spite

The quest for a changeless world is generated in Yeats's poetry by the awareness of living in a mythless culture. But that awareness is itself accompanied by the recognition that nature tends to annihilate man's attempts to find meaning in the exterior world. "The Song of the Happy Shepherd" deals with this pastness of myth and the poet's attempt to re-establish meaning through song. "The Sad Shepherd," its Blakean counterpart, shows the poetic creation being drowned by the natural world.

The old myths that sustained a bygone culture are seen in the first poem as dreams, diversions from the "grey truth" of the present. Truth is not particularly valid here. It is certainly not sufficient to redeem the dead woods or to transform the "dreary dance" or the "cracked tune" of time. Yeats begins, like Stevens, to seek in the present desolation what may suffice, and also like Stevens he affirms the capacity of the poetic word to create and sustain the meaning that is lacking.

"The Song of the Happy Shepherd" offers perhaps too easy a solution. The kings of the old time are kept alive by some idle word some stammering schoolboy repeats. No more profound or enlightening than Shelley's "Ozymandias," Yeats's initial argument deals with the potential of words to transcend time.

The second stanza rejects "dusty deeds" that disappear in time and directs the protagonist to find, in nature, an "echo-harbouring shell" into which he can voice a human song: "Go gather by the humming sea / Some twisted, echo-harbouring shell." Finally, the shepherd will sing to a nature that is both dead and alive—"a

grave / Where daffodil and lily wave," where time does not exist.
The tension between the temporal and the natural that we find in
Wordsworth appears briefly in the last stanza, and the protagonist depicts a world in which death is viewed from Lucy's perspective of nature.

"The Sad Shepherd" discovers that nature does indeed betray
the heart that loves her. He tries to force nature to listen to his
human song, going from sea to meadow and back to the sea. But
the shell, which in the first poem is supposed to echo back to the
human self the tale by which he finds his being, utters instead the
sound of the sea in which the song is drowned. The song which
the singer utters silently in this poem is a conscious creation, an
expression of the self's subjectivity. If nature can indeed re-echo
this song, the tale of woe will reach the singer no longer as a
creation of his consciousness but as an objective description of the
self. The singer would then become creator of the song and
created by it, the place where subjectivity and objectivity are
synthesized. The "ancient burden" of the dialectic between consciousness and reality, which causes the fall from myth, would
"depart," and the self would become the "single light" of
"Solomon and the Witch," the "radical innocence" of "A Prayer
for My Daughter." But again, nature refuses here to be synthesized
or even engaged by the human consciousness. The sea overwhelms
and engulfs the singer by drowning instead of echoing his song,
and nature "forgets" the self who sings to be remembered.

In "The Idea of Order at Key West" Stevens uses the human
voice—the girl's song—as a bridge between the poet's consciousness and the exterior world. Her song, unuttered in the poem,
will both humanize the ocean and allow it to retain its integrity
and its "in-itselfness." But in "Key West" Stevens has already
come to understand that the problem of the imagination is not
that it cannot transform the world, but that it can do so all too
easily, and thus annihilate it. The inarticulate moan of the sea in
Yeats's poem is thus more negative and more far reaching. What
is at stake is not the poet's transformation of the world, but the
existence of poetry itself. In Stevens' poetry the world appears

even more fragile than the poem, and the danger lies in the poet's fragmenting and patching the natural into an intentional and lifeless perspective. In the early Yeats the poem is constantly assailed by the outside world; and because of this tenuousness, this fragility of the poetic structure, he attempts to construct a world "in nature's spite," complete within itself and impervious to the changes of nature or of time. In his attempt to create a world which is perfect and enduring, the natural perspective becomes subsumed within the temporal, and both nature and time are opposed by the intentional, self-contained world of the poem. The poet wants to rebuild unshapely things, but to build them anew he must "sit on a green knoll apart, / With the earth and the sky and the water, remade, like a casket of gold" (*CP*, 54). Like Stevens, or at least like some of Stevens' protagonists such as Hoon, Yeats wants to re-create the world which he inhabits, or rather, to create the world anew and inhabit, in the fullness of being, a world thus intentionally created. But the dialectic which ceases to operate between nature and time operates even more forcefully between the self-conscious creation and the natural though unshapely world. The poet may sit on a green knoll, but it is "a green knoll apart." And the natural world is transmuted into a casket which is a symbol both of intemporality and of death. The intentional creation becomes an act of withdrawal and enclosure, and the successful rebuilding of the outside world ends in the destruction of the world and the imagination that rebuilds it. The casket of gold may seem too extreme an image here. Yet is it not unlike the mechanical golden bird that appears at the end of "Sailing to Byzantium" as a symbol of an imagination that has lost its capacity to sing. The mind which in Wordsworth's *Prelude* is "debarred from Nature's living images" is debarred precisely because it is "compelled to be a life unto herself," in nature's spite.

This dialectic between the natural and the intentional operates quite clearly in "The Two Trees":

> Beloved, gaze in thine own heart,
> The holy tree is growing there.

The natural object in this poem is to be found by a movement inward. As in Rilke, where the poet looks outward but the tree is growing within ("Ich seh hinaus, und in mir wächst der Baum"),[16] we find in this poem a natural process taking place within the confines of an intentional world. Yet the first stanza witnesses a movement outward from this tree. The inner tree, in fact, informs the outer world. Its hidden root "plants" quiet in the night, and the metaphor of an organic process moves paradoxically from the inner structure in which the object is posed metaphorically as something other than itself, out into the natural world where the organic process belongs. The ontological values have not been reversed, but the two processes of generation—the natural and the intentional—have changed sides.[17] What is striking in this poem is not the existence of an inner tree, but the compulsion of the first stanza to effect a comparison between the inner and outer worlds in terms of an organic process which could not possibly be taking place in the inner world in which it is placed. We may say, of course, that the metaphors are all too obvious and stilted: "From joy the holy branches start, / And all the trembling flowers they bear." But through this organic process the tree gives a certain rootedness to existence; it gives order and meaning and centrality to the night. Stevens too, in the early poetry, will look for a symbol which can give order and meaning to the "slovenly wilderness" outside. But he comes up with an intentional construct, a jar that is gray and bare, incapable of bringing into being a meaningful order because incapable, ultimately, of giving of bird or bush. This inner tree in Yeats's poem is perhaps a more felicitous symbol for bridging the distance between the natural and the intentional. Its inner rhythm extends to and engulfs the outer world in "ignorant leafy ways," consciously created perhaps, but organically ignorant of their own growth.

That the tree can be both organic and intentional—consciously created by the poet yet validly informing and transforming the

16. "Es winkt zu Fühlung," *Letzte Gedichte.*
17. See de Man's "Intentional Structure of the Romantic Image" in *Romanticism and Consciousness,* pp. 65–77.

outside world—points to the ability of the protagonist to become the song that he is singing, to transcend the distance between the natural object and the conscious creation by paradoxically including himself within the world transformed by the inner tree he has created. The tree has "dowered the stars with merry light" and "given the waves their melody," but more important it has "made [the poet's] lips and music wed," so that his singing is as natural and unselfconscious as the song of Wordsworth's solitary reaper or the girl's song in Stevens' "Key West," and as the movement of the tree itself. Yeats quite often deals with this capacity of an isolated entity to become one with the framework that contains it ("Who can distinguish darkness from the soul?") or with the medium through which it finds expression ("How can we know the dancer from the dance?"). These instances once again point to the poet's need to transcend the consciousness which invalidates his creations, to bridge the gap between the natural and the intentional and find himself in a place where he can be fully himself and his world. This attempt to create and be one's creation is only another way of arriving at the wholeness sought after in "Ego Dominus Tuus," "A Prayer for My Daughter," and "A Dialogue of Self and Soul." The wish to be both knower and known is also the wish to create a world and be that world, creating oneself through one's creation. The poet then becomes, more obviously than with the image of the self in "Ego Dominus Tuus," subject and object of his genesis.

Yet dealing with the quest for the complete self in terms of artistic creation does not lead Yeats beyond the problem of the image in the mirror but back to it. In the major poems about artistic creation the quest for this completeness ends in a distinction between poet and protagonist, the poet creating the poem, and the fictive self trapped within the confines of total objectivity. The dialectic between the creating self and the created world is not resolved and in turn heightens the dialectic already established between the natural and the intentional. In one of his early poems, Rilke, too, raises a shadowy black tree that once created grows and ripens organically:

Und hast die Welt gemacht. Und sie ist gross
und wie ein Wort, das noch im Schweigen reift.

And you have made the world. And it grows,
like a word that only in silence ripens.[18]

But this tree which is both natural and intentional (like the tree
in the first stanza of Yeats's poem) ripens only in silence. And the
poetic imagination, in order to sustain its capacity for speech,
finds that it must let the object go ("lassen sie deine Augen
zärtlich los"), abandon its attempt to sustain any vision of wholeness beyond the moment, that it may continue to sing.

In the second stanza of "The Two Trees," Yeats returns to the
image in the mirror:

> Gaze no more in the bitter glass
> The demons, with their subtle guile,
> Lift up before us when they pass.

It becomes evident here that the image of an inner tree growing
and ripening organically in the first stanza has been used in opposition to the objective, alienating image in the mirror: "There's
a devil in a looking-glass" (*CP,* 112). In "Ego Dominus Tuus"
the image of the self was conceived as a step toward the integrated
self. Here, the emergence of the image points to the breakdown of
the wholeness presumably achieved in the first stanza. The looking
glass gives forth the "fatal image" that forces the self to recognize
its isolation and its dispossession. The "quiet in the night" of the
first stanza turns into the "stormy night," and the hidden root
which generated peace becomes here "roots half hidden under
snows." The metaphors of summer and winter are perhaps too
obvious, but they may be misleading. What the second stanza
arrives at is the recognition that only by turning inward into the
poetic universe can the organic process be found and sustained.
The image in the mirror is usually associated with inwardness
rather than exteriority, but in this poem inwardness is related to
wholeness and organic process, and the image in the mirror rein-

18. "Eingang," *Das Buch der Bilder.*

troduces the dialectic between the subjective and the objective, the imaginative construct and the outside world. When the imagination turns outward in the second stanza, it is rooted in a barren landscape and forced to recognize its subjectivity. The fatality of the image lies precisely in the aspect of self-consciousness which paradoxically emerges here from the outside world. "The ravens of unresting thought" intrude upon the inner world and destroy its unity. The organic process, the ignorant movement, the oneness of creator and creation are to be found in this poem in the intentional structure of the inner world. Outside may lie reality. But outside, assuredly, lies death. Similar to the movement in Stevens' "Domination of Black," where the poet, afraid of reality, closes off the possible openings between the imagination and the outside world, Yeats affirms here the validity of intentional constructs and the necessity to sustain them in opposition to the exteriority by which they are endangered.[19]

There is a similar dramatic turn between inwardness and exteriority in "The Sorrow of Love." In the first stanza the natural world engulfs the human consciousness, blots out "man's image and his cry" (*CP,* 40)—paradoxically so, since it is the poetic consciousness which evokes the harmony that engulfs it. A girl appears in the second stanza and is compared to Odysseus, who returns home, and to Priam, who does not. In the third stanza the literary consciousness forces nature to return upon itself and recompose the human image it had destroyed. The sky is empty, the leaves offer no longer harmony but lamentation, and out of this emptiness and lamentation within nature the human self is restored. Yeats views the relationship between nature and imagination as one of mutual exclusiveness.

Yet even in the first stanza the literary consciousness is so ob-

19. It would be possible to read the poem simply as the discovery of inwardness. The self would be complete in the first stanza, and that completeness broken in the second by the introduction of the image in the mirror. This would perhaps be a more logical reading, since "the ravens of unresting thought" would be contained within the conscious, inner world. But the directive of the poem is to gaze inward, to avoid the image in the mirror which is an image of the self's exteriority.

viously there (brilliant moon, milky sky, famous harmony) that
any harmony achieved is a fiction which the last stanza both
sustains and destroys—sustains in the sense that the last stanza
is equally literary, equally inflated (clamorous eaves, climbing
moon, empty sky), destroys because it recomposes the human
image which in turn generates the literary consciousness of the
poem. "The Sorrow of Love" is a kind of "Mental Traveller" on
a small scale. The presumed dialectical relationship between self
and world is not there at all. What we have instead is a solipsistic
world where the human consciousness creates the images by
which it is presumably engulfed and then proceeds to destroy or
transform those images and regenerate itself out of their destruction or transformation. Odysseus and Priam are perhaps good
examples, respectively, of a consciousness which returns to the point
of origin and sets out again, and a consciousness for which there is
no return. The circular and in fact solipsistic pattern of the poem
elucidates the nature of Odysseus' doom and points to Priam
murdered as a double symbol of an exteriority destroyed (sealing
the "doom" of the poem) and a consciousness destroyed by the
recognition of its solipsism. In this sense Priam becomes the
central figure in a poem that wishes to break through its own
doom and understands that to do so is also to be destroyed.

This ambivalent relationship between imagination and reality
is also explored in "Solomon and the Witch." The witch appears
only in the title, and we are left to decide whether she is the
Sheba of the poem or a figure of the imagination whose precursor
could well be Shelley's "Witch of Atlas." But we have in the
poem two antithetical forces that come together only sexually,
and whose failure to find what Stevens calls "the voice of union"
prompts Sheba's "let us try again." The poem begins *in medias
res,* with Sheba recounting a previous encounter: "I suddenly
cried out in a strange tongue / Not his, not mine." The "strange
tongue" is as ambivalent as the function of the witch. Or rather,
because the poem begins *in medias res,* we have to read on to
interpret whether this strange tongue "not his, not mine" suggests
the consummate marriage of imagination and reality or the in-

ability to utter intelligible speech. In either case (it could be
both) poetic speech is endangered by the imminence of silence.
The cockerel crowing from the blossoming apple bough predicts
the fall from the garden, then the regaining of innocence. But it
is an achieved innocence, a Blakean organized innocence which
no longer depends on the rejection of knowledge but which syn-
thesizes knowledge and life, imagination and reality, choice and
chance, human will and gratuitous existence. Both self and world
become transformed as they reach this identity which does not
reject the previous dialectical stages but contains them and resolves them: "The world ends when these two things, / Though
several, are a single light, / When oil and wick are burned in
one." The imagination seems to be re-entering the garden from
this side of history, forcing the cockerel to conclude that the
redemptive hour has come: "He that crowed out eternity /
Thought to have crowed it in again." Of course, the cockerel is
wrong in thinking that "this foul world [is] dead at last."
Prophetic knowledge is not accessible within the temporal perspective. (The added problem here is that the cockerel thinks that by
prophesying he brings things to pass.) There are only false
prophets in history, whose visions of eternity are generated only
by their will to transcend time. Will is not choice, and ultimately
neither choice nor chance is sufficient to transcend the temporal
perspective: "the world stays." Instead of a marriage between
imagination and reality, "the bride-bed brings despair," disparity,
disunion, reaffirming the dialectical and in a sense asynthetical
relationship: "For each an imagined image brings / And finds a
real image there." The resolution from this point on would
become the resolution of "A Dialogue of Self and Soul" or "Ego
Dominus Tuus," simply rejecting one side of the dialectic rather
than synthesizing it. "Maybe an image is too strong / Or maybe
is not strong enough." The image is too strong because its tendency
is to usurp and destroy the immediacy of the natural object (unlike Ammons' mirror in the weed which mirrors the mirror in the
self mirroring the weed); not strong enough because it cannot, intentionally, create what will suffice. The sacred grove, like

the world, remains. But within it there is only the crushed grass—the evidence of the attempted passage into eternity, seen in its pastness, from the perspective of time.

We have seen the unresolved and, to some extent, hidden dialogue of Self and Soul continued in "Solomon and the Witch," in similar terms and with similar results. In the *Tower* poems, and particularly in "Sailing to Byzantium," Yeats attempts to create the image that is "strong enough," to construct an intentional, intemporal world that will suffice.

"That is no country for old men." The first stanza is perhaps the most ambiguous of the poem, and in that sense the most rewarding. The rest of the poem moves in the direction of an all too simple solution to the problems which generate it and forces a distinction between poet and protagonist which we have seen operating in the Lucy poems. The protagonist moves into a world that is ultimately antithetical to poetic creation. The poet remains on the outside, caught neither in the sensual music of the first stanza nor in the intentional but silent music of the last. Like Wordsworth's "There was a Boy," the poem gets written in an act simultaneously of silence and of speech, with the protagonist trapped in the changeless circle of eternity and the poet still "sailing" from the world of time. The relationship between poet and protagonist is in this sense a reversal of that which we find in Dante's *Comedy* or Hegel's *Phenomenology*. Here poet and protagonist are presumably one in the first stanza, and by the end of the poem the poet discovers what the protagonist, trapped in eternity, cannot know. The "success" of the poem depends to some extent on our reading into it an ironic dimension by which Yeats remains detached from the "solution" which he posits.

If we read the poem in this manner, then the title becomes more intelligible. For by the end of the poem the protagonist cannot involve himself in any action which of necessity must take place within the temporal world. The participial ending of the verb in the title strengthens this sense of process which the protagonist's intemporality at the end of the poem must deny. The poet's is a constant sailing to Byzantium and a constant separation from the protagonist who arrives. To thus read "Sailing to Byzantium" in terms of a circular and never-ending pattern is to read it as a kind of "Mental Traveller." Redemption in Yeats's poem, if indeed it can be called that, lies not in the eternity of Byzantium, but in the constant "sailing to" by which the poet escapes the ficticity and silence of the protagonist in the last stanza.

It is not unusual to find in nineteenth- and twentieth-century poetry a protagonist who creates and whose creation distinguishes him from the poet. Sometimes the protagonist's "creation" is an unselfconscious song—Wordsworth's "Solitary Reaper," Stevens' "Key West"—and in those instances poet and protagonist become distinct in terms of the dialectic between what is natural and what is intentional. Yeats himself will observe this form in "A Crazed Girl." Sometimes, the protagonist creates and inhabits a world to which the poet is denied access, as in Coleridge's "Kubla Khan." This poem is of particular interest here, because in some ways it seems to be a precursor of Yeats's poem; yet "Sailing to Byzantium" is ultimately its reversal. Kubla Khan "decrees" the pleasure dome, creates it by an act of poetic volition, and inhabits the world he has created: a world at the same time walled in yet not dissociated from natural reality (sun, gardens, fertile ground, blossoming trees). In the midst of the sounds of fountains and rivers, he hears a prophecy of war. Yet the prophecy applies not to Kubla Khan's world but to that of the poet, who must wage war on nature to become a prophet of the imagination. At the end of the poem Coleridge contemplates the pleasure dome which his protagonist can both create and inhabit, knowing that he himself is doomed to remain on the outside of what he has created. The protagonist creates himself by creating his world, and between self and world no rift of consciousness intrudes. For the poet, the intrusion of consciousness is not only a fact, but also that which paradoxically redeems the poem from the silence into which it would fall were it to enact its protagonist's success. Poetry is indeed that act of mediation by which the poet is denied access to the world he envisions, but also by virtue of which he continues to sing. At the end of "Kubla Khan" the conditional tense points to the poet's inability to enter the world he has created, and the pleasure dome in which creator and creation would reach a perfect coincidence remains what Eliot calls "a perpetual possibility / Only in a world of speculation."[20] In "Sailing to Byzantium," on the contrary, the poet presumes—though his presumption is also conditioned by the future tense—that the totality of Byzantium is accessible to poetic creation. The poet does not overtly distinguish himself from the protagonist, and at the end of the poem the fictional self has achieved the deadening completeness posited in "A Dialogue of Self and Soul." Inwardness and exteriority are no longer viable categories, but the golden bird, like the Soul in the "Dialogue," is incapable of song.

This oneness framed in a pattern of inaccessibility occurs in "A Crazed Girl":

> That crazed girl improvising her music,
> Her poetry, dancing upon the shore.

The madness of the protagonist provides the occasion for an extreme and intimate relationship between her and reality, or is perhaps the result of such a relationship. The music she creates is exactly the opposite of the poet's intentional construct. It is "improvised," an unselfconscious expression which links rather than distances the protagonist from her world. Her dancing reaffirms this oneness and places her in a world complete within itself, which the poet may contemplate but into which he cannot enter— a world from which, like Wordsworth, he must gently pass. The protagonist, however, is not outside the temporal perspective. She is caught in it, "in desperate music wound," yet also transcends it through her music ("no matter what disaster occurred"). Her song, her dancing, and her madness reveal her as both touched and untouched by time, caught in the space in which she dances, but at the same time triumphing over the poet's dualistic world. Her words "O sea-starved, hungry sea" suggest a reality that

20. *Four Quartets,* "Burnt Norton," I.

reverts upon itself (sea starved for the sea) and mirrors both the oneness of the crazed girl and the music and the poet's hunger for that oneness. The poet tries to render the protagonist's reality accessible by transforming the sound which is "no common intelligible sound" into human speech. This act of translation distinguishes Yeats's poem from Stevens' "Key West," or Wordsworth's "Solitary Reaper," or Coleridge's "Kubla Khan." In uttering the unintelligible and the unspeakable, the poet destroys the possible center of silence of the poem and paradoxically renders even more inaccessible the world into which he seems to step. "It is not that words *cannot* say / what is missing: it is only that what is missing / cannot / be missed if / spoken."[21] There is in Yeats an obsession to contain all worlds, to create the work beyond which there is nothing, and at the same time a recognition, though not as central and persistent as Ammons' or Stevens' recognition, of the limited dimensions of poetic speech.

In "Sailing to Byzantium" the protagonist passes into a different kind of silence, one generated not by his proximity to reality but by his unqualified affirmation of the value of poetic speech and the eternal world it can create. The first stanza presents a cyclical and self-contained world of nature constantly regenerating itself: the "dying generations" die only to be reborn. The gerundive form, repeating the participial ending of the title, underlines the repetitive, ongoing process within the natural perspective and points to the profusion of a summer world which inevitably returns to summer. This natural world is one of song and sensual music which celebrates its own fulfillment—a timeless world to some extent, yet defined by a temporal inevitability. "Whatever is begotten, born, and dies" reveals an endlessly recurring pattern that cannot help its own recurrence. The "and" suggests nature's inevitable passage back into itself and points both to the entrapment of the human in this profusion of the natural ("Caught in that sensual music all neglect . . .") and to the protagonist's isolation ("That is no country for old men").

Assailed by this consciousness of aging, the protagonist seeks

---

21. A. R. Ammons, "Unsaid," *Selected Poems*.

the "monuments of unageing intellect" forgotten in the first stanza. The second stanza picks up the image of these monuments reverting on themselves (like nature in the first stanza or the sea in "A Crazed Girl"), studying and affirming their own magnificence. The transcendence of the temporal is thus conceived in terms of an art that sings about itself, that takes itself for its own subject, creating a realm as complete and permanent as— more permanent than—that of nature. Byzantium is in this sense a place that generates itself, mirroring itself as cause and consequence of its genesis. The poet, at the end of the second stanza, has presumably arrived, or at least seems to stand on the threshold of this self-contained and self-sustaining world. To enter into it, he has to fully transcend the natural, to be gathered "into the artifice of eternity." Art is conceived here in opposition to both the temporal and the natural, and the dramatic turn occurs when the poet recognizes that he may, perhaps, create "in nature's spite," but not in an eternal world.

The identity of nature and time is affirmed in the third stanza. One premise of the poem is that nature and art are mutually exclusive, a premise which Wordsworth is careful not to carry too far and which Stevens eventually rejects. The poet conceives of himself in this stanza as a "dying animal," but without the capacity of the "dying generations" of the first stanza to transcend his temporal finiteness. Rather, those dying generations can transcend their finiteness because they are unaware of it. But the poet views both the temporal and the natural perspectives as processes in which the self is caught against its will and in which it dies. Fully in the Blakean tradition in this respect, the poetic imagination wishes to disengage itself from the domain of change. Though nature is described in terms of permanence in the first stanza, Yeats ends by conceiving it in terms of time, a time which regenerates the natural perhaps, but which forces upon the poet a process of disintegration. To be "natural" is to be "dying," a state in which the self "knows not what it is." To discover itself, to create itself out of itself, it must pass fully "out of nature." The poet wants to become himself a work of art, no longer dying in the world of time but possessing the necessity of an intentional structure. In the last stanza, he achieves (though in the future tense) this desired completeness, but the self is at the same time eternalized and reduced, trapped in a changeless world more deathlike than that of the "dying generations." The song of the natural in the first stanza, transmuted in the second stanza into a song singing of itself—singing itself—and thus transcending its mortality, becomes in the last stanza an unsung song, the virtual song of the mechanical bird which can sing "of what is past, or passing, or to come." Nature in "The Sad Shepherd" annihilated human song. Here, the human song is sung in nature's spite and transcends indeed its own humanity. The temporal inevitability of process in the first stanza ("whatever is begotten, born, *and* dies"), becomes in the last an indifference and imperviousness to time. The "or" points to the self's transcendence of the temporal-natural process, but it points also to the self's inability to sing. The containment of time within the song (what is past, or passing, or to come) precludes the enactment of the song in time (a situation which "Lapis Lazuli" will reverse) and signals the silencing of the poetic self.

It is here, of course, that we may separate poet and protagonist (unless we take the future tense to mean desirability but not achievement of Byzantium). For the poet creates a poem about the death of creativity, about a self that seeks to generate itself and dies into eternity. The protagonist becomes in the last stanza an art-object, achieving eternity at the price of the subjectivity which at the same time generates the desire for eternity and creates the poem that achieves it. The poet-in-the-poem thus reaches totality by an objectification of the self (the "happily I am completely dead" of Mallarmé), but it is a totality in which, as in "A Dialogue of Self and Soul," his "tongue's a stone." The protagonist at the end of the poem conceives himself beyond the temporal and the natural, beyond the world of change. Yet we are reminded, by the future tense which prevails in the last stanza (prefaced by the imperative in the third), that the poet's achievement is a hypothetical one, or rather that the protagonist achieves a wholeness which silences his capacity for creation but which allows the poet to create a poem about the drive toward an eternal world and a repeated "sailing to." That the poem can be read in terms of a circular structure is what redeems the poet from the fate of his protagonist. This reading also allows us to return to the first line—"That is no country for old men"—and to interpret it not only in terms of a natural world from which the poet is cast out, but also in terms of this final vision of Byzantium from which he chooses to withdraw. In this ironic dimension lies Yeats's paradoxical affirmation of the temporal perspective which he ostensibly, through the poem, wishes to transcend.

This return to the temporal occurs, in nineteenth- and twentieth-century poetry, in poems that affirm the value of a changeless world as well as in those that affirm the value of the natural perspective. In "Ode to a Nightingale" Keats is tempted to pursue the bird "over the still stream," yet recognizes the danger of being lost to the world in which poetry is possible. He thus chooses to remain, to be tolled back to his "sole self." He affirms at the end of the "Ode" the temporal perspective from which he writes the poem and refuses to be engulfed by the world of process which the nightingale inhabits. Yeats affirms, in the title of his poem, the temporal perspective, and refuses to purchase the vision of wholeness at the price of creativity which his protagonist pays.

If we do not distinguish poet and protagonist, we may of course see in "Sailing to Byzantium" a purgatorial pattern not unlike that of "The Rime of the Ancient Mariner," in which the self never breaks through into a vision of eternity. The poet would thus repeat interminably the act of sailing to Byzantium, the way the mariner must endlessly repeat his tale. Both would know that "redemption" is only a fictive possibility. Yet we often find Yeats rebelling against the limitations of poetry, against his inability to contain or establish contact with the outside world:

> The swan has leaped into the desolate heaven:
> That image can bring wildness, bring a rage
> To end all things, to end

What my laborious life imagined, even
The half-imagined, the half-written page.
                        ["Nineteen Hundred and Nineteen"]

The desolate heaven mirrors the desolation of the imagined, and
the profound dissatisfaction with poetic creation turns into a desire for decreation. But a poetry that turns upon itself and wishes
to unwrite what has been written is a poetry that validates reality
more than it cares, in Yeats's world, to admit.

The Vision of History

From "Sailing to Byzantium" to "Byzantium" we can trace a
passage from the quest for the finished and intemporal creation
(and the concomitant objectification of the self) to a quest for
the process of creation, in which the self, within time, simultaneously creates and destroys the images that would allow it to
pass into eternity.

"The unpurged images of day recede." The first stanza witnesses a natural passage into darkness (twilight hour) and
simultaneously a passage from the natural to the intentional and
the imaginative. Day's images are unpurged, gratuitous, beset by
the complexities of human time—"the fury and the mire of human veins." As they recede, the imagination (starlit or moonlit
dome) conceives a world no longer gratuitous but intentional,
purged of its historical and temporal complexity. The process is
not one-sided, however. We may argue that imagination arises
because the unpurged images recede, but it is equally possible—
perhaps even more feasible—to argue that the imagination forces
those unpurged images to recede and in darkness creates a world
distinct from nature and time. The question raised in the "Dialogue"—"who can distinguish darkness from the soul"—is ap-
plicable to some extent to the imagination's perspective. Like
Stevens speaking of the "rugged black" of the intentional image,
Yeats sees the imagination in this poem creating from darkness
(creating darkness in fact) a world of self-begotten flames.

There seems to be, at least initially in this poem, a quest for purity, for the image that generates itself, a quest in fact for the self who becomes both cause and consequence of itself, transforming the dialogue of self and soul into a monologue where all dialectics are synthesized and all complexities dissolved. "Byzantium" too involves the danger of an art that in its desire for the absolute rejects its humanity ("all that man is") and reduces itself to silence. The poet conceives himself as dead in the second stanza, and therefore able to call forth images and shades: "A mouth that has no moisture and no breath / Breathless mouths may summon." He has dissociated himself from the world of living things in entering or creating Byzantium, and the world of art coincides with the world of the living dead. Those dead to the living world come alive in Byzantium, and death-in-life *becomes* life-in-death, a form of artistic resurrection, of imaginative, "superhuman" rebirth. The poet who has rejected the complexities of history, who is in fact metaphorically dead to the natural and the temporal, is able by virtue of his estrangement to call forth the image of himself, "shade more than man, more image than a shade"; to achieve, circularly, the completeness he must possess to call forth and assume the shade.

The bird in the third stanza (reminiscent of the golden bird of "Sailing to Byzantium") is neither a living bird nor a silent art-object. "More miracle than bird or handiwork," it pertains to an imaginative world which simultaneously functions as organically as the natural and rejects once again the complexities of mire and blood with which the natural is associated. The bird is "planted" on the starlit golden bough, it can utter sounds, it can "like the cocks of Hades crow." But the sounds it utters are related to the living dead of the second stanza, alive because dead, impervious to historical complexities. The bird, like the poet, "scorn[s] aloud / In glory of changeless metal / Common bird or petal / And all complexities of mire or blood." Byzantium is a place where being is purchased at the price of the becoming and where the miracle of the imagination is "embittered" by the moon.[22] The imagination passes here from the natural and the temporal into the eternal, into a world that, purified of the becoming, reaches into itself (like nature in the first stanza of "Sailing to Byzantium") and generates itself.

"Ein Rätsel ist Reinentsprungenes" (an enigma is something of pure origin),[23] says Hölderlin. The fourth stanza of "Byzantium" projects the imagination into this "pure" world, a world which it creates and in which it simultaneously creates itself. The self-generating flames—"flames begotten of flame"—bespeak this totality, this absoluteness of a self that has moved out of the temporal realm, into a world in which it discovers itself as the origin both of itself and of its world. The flames spring from nothing, from the emperor's pavement, "flames that no faggot feeds, nor steel has lit." The poetic imagination contemplates here its moment of origin and achieves through this contemplation a vision of unity and simplicity that does not oppose itself to the complexities of nature and time and history but contains and resolves them. "All complexities of fury leave," and the self discovers (and participates in) its own genesis.

The passage into this moment of origin is given through the rituals of dance and flame—rites of passage, of purification, also of self-forgetfulness. Remembrance and forgetfulness, however, are not dialectical except in time. The self that passes into being forgets itself but passes into itself, remembers itself in a moment which is timeless because it is itself the origin of time. Thus what seems to be an affirmation of intemporality, a quest for eternity, is revealed in this fourth stanza as an affirmation of time. Precisely because the poem moves into the moment of origin of Byzantium, and consequently into its own moment of origin, it reaffirms the temporal perspective which allows it to exist. In a sense, the previous "sailing to" Byzantium both succeeds and fails

22. Embittered probably because the moon changes, and it cannot change.
23. "Der Rhein."

here, because the arrival is an arrival in a world that is not intemporal, but ultimately involved with time. Where Stevens will
create, or discover, an eternal moment at the very center of the
temporal perspective, Yeats discovers, or creates, at the center of
eternity, a passage back into the world of time. There is no longer
any need to reaffirm temporality in terms of a direction, a "sailing to." Temporality lies at the very center of the poem, in terms
of rituals that of necessity must be enacted in time, but also in
terms of a self that in discovering its absoluteness discovers also its
involvement with the historical perspective.

This simultaneity of history and eternity is reaffirmed in the last
stanza. The smithies of the emperor "break" the flood of history,
but as Bloom points out "break" has more than one meaning.[24]
The smithies "break bitter furies of complexity" in the sense that
they destroy complexity by the achieved vision of simplicity, but
also in the sense that they create it by multiplying the complexities
that already exist. "Images that yet / Fresh images beget" are
wrought out of the fourth stanza's discovery of origin, but also
out of the fifth stanza's recognition that origin is involved with
history. The complexities of the temporal are both affirmed and
transcended, and more important they are affirmed even in the
self's transcendence of them. Apparently a poem that thrusts the
protagonist into a timeless world. "Byzantium" becomes a poem
in which the protagonist rediscovers time at the very center of the
intemporal, and reaffirms it. The distinction between poet and
protagonist, which was essential to the survival of the poet in
"Sailing to Byzantium," is no longer necessary here, and in fact
no longer possible. The poem that contains within itself its own
origin, that is created by an imaginative act toward the intemporal which ends by discovering its own temporality, becomes
both Byzantium and a rite of passage into Byzantium—the means
toward the experience and the experience itself.

The *Last Poems* reaffirm the relationship, achieved in "Byzan-

24. "In 'Byzantium' 'break' seems to mean both 'mar' and 'create'"
(*Yeats,* p. 392).

tium," between the intentional and the historical, between the work of art and the temporal-natural perspective. This relationship is perhaps most evident in "The Gyres" and "Lapis Lazuli," though neither poem is as successful structurally, as self-contained as "Byzantium." In "Byzantium" the discovery of the validity of the temporal occurs within the poem—the process by which such a "revelation" is arrived at is built into the poem's structure. "The Gyres" begins already with a knowledge of such validity, and as a result it is more philosophical and less exciting in terms of the "happening" of the poem. The spiraling movement of the gyres signifies the quest for history—for the valid moment *in* time. "Things thought too long can be no longer thought, / For beauty dies of beauty, worth of worth." Thought and beauty, if conceived as intemporal, self-sustaining categories, destroy themselves through the very eternity that prevents their temporal destruction. This theme of the danger of the intemporal is not at all unusual in nineteenth-century poetry, and it flourishes in the twentieth century. In "La Statue" Baudelaire speaks of a statue whose empty eyes mirror the eternal but are unable for that reason to focus on the temporal, and they miss thus the presentness of things. The dialectic between the temporal and the eternal is brought out by Yeats as well on a number of occasions. He speaks of a beauty "grown sad with its eternity" (*CP*, 38), a phantom "ever pacing on the verge of things" (*CP*, 12). The beauty conceived in its eternity is unable to relate to the particular, unable in fact to actualize itself in time. In an early poem, "The Living Beauty," Yeats speaks of having attempted to

> draw content
> From beauty that is cast out of a mould
> In bronze, or that in dazzling marble appears,
> Appears, but when we have gone is gone again,
> Being more indifferent to our solitude
> Than 'twere an apparition.

Attempting to validate a changeless world, he recognizes that the absolute is indifferent to our humanity ("when we have gone is gone again"), and that its contemplation makes us feel more

lonely and estranged than before. In yet another poem, "The
Statues" (included in the *Last Poems*), he speaks of "empty eyeballs" for whom "knowledge increases unreality" and "mirror on
mirror mirrored is all the show." The knowledge of eternity is not
redemption but damnation—a knowledge which "increases unreality," which divorces us from the immediacy of things. The
empty eyeballs of Yeats's statue focus not on the temporal, not
even on the eternal, but on the statue itself, and the infinite
mirroring of images initiated out of a quest for unity ends in a
reassertion of self-consciousness and a further splintering of the
self: "The mirror-scalèd serpent is multiplicity" (*CP*, 283). The
mirror, which initially fascinates Yeats as an instrument of totality
and self-revelation, ends as a metaphysical trap that locks us in
the consequences of the fall. "Things thought too long can be no
longer thought, / For beauty dies of beauty, worth of worth."
Thought exhausts itself in its very inexhaustibility, and beauty
dies paradoxically in its deathlessness, a deathlessness which is not
immortality but merely deadness, an imperviousness to the living
and changing world.

"The Gyres" attempts to force the beauty locked in its eternity
to spiral downward into the world of time, into the "irrational
streams" and complexities of history. Because deathlessness is the
true damnation, history in this poem is not only tragic but
joyful. Or at least every historical moment becomes for Yeats an
occasion for tragic joy. The historical instant is validated in and
for itself. Eternity, beauty, all categories of the absolute must
actualize themselves, "wither into the truth" (*CP*, 92). Where
Keats posits an absolute relationship between truth and beauty,
Yeats conceives of truth as a withering process by which the
"fictive covering" (as Stevens will call it) of intemporality is dis-
posed of and its essential temporality revealed. Thus the poet no
longer tries to escape the process of history in which tragedy occurs.
The second stanza reaffirms the validity of this process, as irrational as such a process may appear. The body is "sensitive" to
the blood and mire which "Byzantium" both transcended and restored. The poet rejects the ancient tombs whose art was to

preserve the imitation of life and impelled by the word "rejoice" spirals out of eternity and into history. The cavern of the second stanza, like the broken sepulchre of the third, suggests this opening up of the intentional structure, this movement out of the ancient tombs in an affirmation of the capacity for resurrection. Resurrection is not *beyond* history, but *within* it. The poet creates no longer a changeless world which like the boxes of make-up gives what is dead the appearance of life, but creates out of the material of history—the marble of a broken sepulchre or "any rich, dark nothing." Imaginative redemption is associated not with the completed and timeless form but with the pieces of marble that come from the broken form, from the sepulchre which, broken, leads to life. The poet does not create out of nothing, or out of his imagination's need to escape time, but "disinters" what is there ("[from] any rich, dark nothing disinter"), the verb suggesting both an imaginative resurrection and a reaffirmation of the imagination's involvement with the temporal world.

"The Gyres" begins from a view of eternity and passes into history. "Lapis Lazuli" begins from history and passes into a perspective of eternity which, as in "Byzantium," validates the temporality which was the starting point. It is possible to see this poem divided into two unintegrated parts, one dealing with history, the other with the art-object. Yet the last part of the poem meditates on and contains the first, so that the historical perspective is reaffirmed within the vision that presumably transcends it.[25] The opening stanza presents history as the domain of meaninglessness—a fragmentary world in which art has lost the capacity to make sense, to create a center of order. Reminiscent of the women who come and go talking of Michelangelo in "The Love Song of J. Alfred Prufrock," the women, hysterical, watch a civilization's downfall and voice their disgust with the ineffective-

25. In the 1938 printing of the poem in *The New Republic* (April 13, 1938), the fourth stanza was not separated from the third. See *The Variorum Edition of the Poems of W. B. Yeats,* ed. Peter Allt and Russell K. Alspach (New York: Macmillan, 1957).

ness of art to counteract it. We may well return here to Yeats's
concept of art in the ancient world. That singleness of vision, that
unified perspective which made of the artist an artisan, and
brought into being a vision of reality whose existence tautologically
reaffirmed the unity from which it sprang, is totally absent in the
modern world. Poetry of course may try to re-create, intentionally
and fictively, the unity of being of the ancient Byzantium. That
possibility is not even dealt with in this poem. Poetry may also disregard reality, be gay by ignoring catastrophe. Or it may, as
"Byzantium" intimated and "Lapis Lazuli" explicitly points out,
achieve gaiety out of the acknowledgment of catastrophe and the
possibility of beginning again. The last stanza in fact will deal, as
did "Byzantium," with the very origin of the act which allows
both music and poem, and in fact civilization itself, to begin
again. What we have in "Lapis Lazuli" is a recognition of the
futility of an art that wills itself intemporal. The women who are
sick of the palette and fiddle bow are hysterical only because they
do not understand the nature of their objections. But their objections are well founded. Poetry is not redeemed from history by
ignoring it, but by coming to terms with temporality, by "disin-
terring" both from the past and from the present the knowledge
that allows us to begin again.

This knowledge, however, is derived from a vision in which
history is less gratuitous than the first stanza would seem to indicate, a vision in which history is seen more as a performance leading to a well-known end than as an acceptance of absurdity. Perhaps the certainty of destruction and despair is what provides
within the historical perspective the well-known end that makes
gaiety—tragic joy—a possibility. The recognition of a pattern in
history which leads from civilization to destruction and back again
to civilization provides a framework as ordered and as "necessary"
as that of a play and creates, within this framework, the occasion
for tragic joy. What the imagination "disinters" in "The Gyres"
is not so much fragments of the past (Eliot's fragments shored

against the ruins),[26] but the knowledge of a pattern which those
fragments are witness to. The "tragic play" is not only Lear's and
Cordelia's. The "they" of the fourth line in the second stanza
refers both to the characters in the play and to the actors playing
their parts. The confusion is intentional, and necessary. The
knowledge that the actors have of the final scene, as well as
the wisdom about life and the insight into tragedy that the tragic
characters acquire before the end, transforms both dread and
absurdity into a joy as irrational as the events that befall them.
This stanza suggests that the joy is not irrational, that the pattern
of tragedy, which is also the pattern of civilizations, justifies it.
"Tragedy wrought to its uttermost" leads into this insight which
if not comic provides at least the framework for an inner transformation. The play "cannot grow by an inch or an ounce," yet
its intentional pattern is not all that different from the pattern of
history: "All things fall and are built again, / And those that
build them again are gay."

> Two Chinamen, behind them a third,
> Are carved in lapis lazuli,
> Over them flies a long-legged bird,
> A symbol of longevity;
> The third, doubtless a serving-man,
> Carries a musical instrument.
>
> Every discoloration of the stone,
> Every accidental crack or dent,
> Seems a water-course or an avalanche,
> Or lofty slope where it still snows
> Though doubtless plum or cherry-branch
> Sweetens the little half-way house
> Those Chinamen climb towards, and I
> Delight to imagine them seated there;
> There, on the mountain and the sky,
> On all the tragic scene they stare.
> One asks for mournful melodies;

26. *The Waste Land:* "These fragments I have shored against my
ruins."

Accomplished fingers begin to play.
Their eyes mid many wrinkles, their eyes,
Their ancient, glittering eyes, are gay.

The work of art is thus introduced into the poem as part of this historical perspective, as an occurrence within it. And the relationship between the content of the art-object (its vision of itself and of history) and the historical perspective which generates it becomes the subject of a poem that infinitely mirrors its own genesis. What is particularly interesting about "Lapis Lazuli" is that the poem, taking itself for its own subject by positing within itself another intentional structure which in turn posits another (the music about to be played), does not separate itself from history by creating a static and enclosed world. All to the contrary, we find in the world of the lapis a vision of history that contains destruction and creation and at the end produces the same gaiety of those who in history begin to rebuild again. The Chinamen at the end—playing and listening to the music—are performing their roles in a perspective that is no longer artistic, enclosed within an intentional world, but temporal and therefore historical. Their gaiety relates them to the builders of fallen civilizations and becomes in turn the link between the vision of art and the vision of history which precedes it. We may say indeed that this joy which functions as a link between the artistic and the historical becomes the subject of a poem that attempts precisely to link these two disparate perspectives. To state the existence of such a relationship is not sufficient. The first three stanzas of the poem did that, yet all the examples from tragedy still required an enactment—an act of gaiety and of initiation—within the poem itself. The gaiety of the last stanza answers the hysteria of the first and affirms the temporality within which the initiation must take place.

That it does occur places "Lapis Lazuli" within the tradition of "Byzantium," as a poem containing within itself its own origin, its own moment of genesis. Yet "Byzantium" is less concerned with history as a pattern of human events. In "Byzantium" Yeats affirms the imagination's involvement with temporality by placing the origin of the poem at its center. The poem, thus, becomes enactment. The last two stanzas of "Lapis Lazuli" repeat the structure of "Byzantium," but relating this enactment to a larger and in a sense more clearly present temporal perspective. The repetition of the poem's act of creation within the poem is also the repetition of creation within history. In fact, we witness a curious and fascinating identity between the two creative acts: as if, simultaneously, we could conceive of the poem being created by history and in turn creating history; rebuilding civilization, and being in turn rebuilt. The act within the poem that constantly generates it also extends to the vision of history the poem posits but within which it is contained. The poem and the world, the intentional and the historical, coincide, and the creation of the poem integrates the poet to the historical process he contemplates.

Such attempted coincidences of the intentional structure and the exterior world are rather common in literature. We find, indeed, three instances in Stevens' poetry—"The Reader," "The House Was Quiet and the World Was Calm," and "Three Travelers Watch a Sunrise"—in which an attempt is made to create a passage between the work and the world, and through that passage reach identity. Yet these works fail because they do not contain their own act of creation, and so the attempted identity ends with the intentional structure containing and fictionalizing the exterior world. In "Lapis Lazuli" the poem does indeed contain the outside world, as well as itself. But it also contains its own origin and affirms the temporality which both creates it from within and destroys it from without.

We can now look at how the poem arrives at this moment of genesis within itself. The framework within the framework alone, as we have seen, will not achieve this. In fact, for the twentieth century the contemplation of an artistic structure within another artistic structure is not unusual. What is unusual is the reversion of this structure upon itself and its affirmation of a world of process which of necessity lies outside its confines. This affirmation of process, of temporality within an intemporal structure, makes possible the enactment of the music—the accomplished

fingers actually begin to play—and leads the poem into a contemplation both of its own origin and of its place in history. On
the one hand, the lapis (a very hard stone) and the figures on it
(carved) are presented as escaping or contradicting the very
obvious effects of temporality in the preceding stanzas. Yet the
introduction of the musical instrument creates the possibility of a
temporal process within the art-object. This possibility, of course,
is very tenuous. A similar situation is repeated in Keats's "Ode on
a Grecian Urn," but there time is denied access to the structure
on which the poem meditates, and the music is present only
theoretically, as "ditties of no tone." Keats in fact validates the
intemporality of this structure, the "foreverness" of the poses, and
the eternal virtuality of the music. The creative act in the "Ode"
is forever about to take place and, temporally absent from the
poem, it detracts as well from the poem's capacity for enactment.
The questions raised in the first stanza of Keats's poem, and which
point to the spectator's inability to enter the world he is contemplating, lead to the object's refusal to reveal itself in the
fourth. The town and its streets "for evermore / Will silent be;
and not a soul to tell / Why thou art desolate, can e'er return."
The meditation of one artistic structure on another does not in
this case become mediation but withdrawal, and the "cold
pastoral" applies to both the silent urn and the poem which
cannot penetrate its (the urn's and its own) silence. In the final
analysis, the creative act that is never arrived at in Keats's poem
does not "tease us out of thought" but into it, and the "truth"
the poet seeks remains distinct from the temporality which would
enact it.

The apparent similarities between Keats's "Ode" and Yeats's
poem belie not only major differences but opposing principles.
The beginning of the last stanza in "Lapis Lazuli" thrusts time
into the world of the lapis. This hard and durable stone, its
durability underscored by the "symbol of longevity" which it
contains, is itself transformed by a world of time and process
which lies outside its intentional confines and whose existence
cannot be refuted or ignored. Neither the poem nor the lapis

wishes to ignore it. In fact the affirmation of temporality thrusts the lapis into its own moment of creation, allowing movement to take place (the Chinamen, unlike the figures in Keats's poem, climb toward the halfway house) and the music to begin. Indeed, the temporality which lies outside the lapis and affects it is itself transmuted into a natural perspective which is both temporal and timeless and within which movement and enactment are real possibilities: "Every discoloration of the stone, / Every accidental crack or dent, / Seems a water-course or an avalanche, / Or lofty slope where it still snows." The discolorations, cracks, and dents— the visible "proofs" of temporality on the art-object—become in turn a natural landscape in the structure, a landscape in which the natural and the temporal work together to make possible, within the poem, the enactment of the poetic act. The dialectic between the intentional and the natural is totally dissolved here. The intentional *becomes* the natural, and time is the agent of mediation. The temporality which was affirmed as exterior to the lapis becomes also affirmed within the natural landscape of the lapis (a landscape, as we have said, paradoxically created by time itself), and this makes possible the movement of the figures toward the house and ultimately the initiation of the music itself.

Viewed in this way, the lofty slope where it still snows becomes an affirmation both of temporality (circularly, because the affirmation of temporality is what allows it to snow) and of permanence (because it "still" snows). This permanence in process, which David Perkins finds in the greater romantics,[27] occurs in Yeats's poem within the artistic structure and in turn projects the sense of process and permanence, change and continuity, on to the historical perspective itself. Or rather, the temporality that floods the intentional structure and makes possible the temporal-natural process within it is reflected back into the temporal-historical perspective in terms of a permanence which was already there, but not paradigmatically understood. Longevity seems a foolish

27. David Perkins, *The Quest for Permanence: The Symbolism of Wordsworth, Shelley, and Keats* (Cambridge: Harvard University Press, 1959), esp. p. 33.

word to use considering the vision of history that precedes it. Yet it preludes and is explained by the paradoxical validation of the temporal perspective within the art-object in the following stanza. The fourth stanza, in this sense, begins as a carry-over from the third, introducing into the lapis figures that might well have belonged to the windswept generations of the preceding stanza. In the fifth stanza these figures look back upon the historical perspective they have left, and like the actors in the plays, like the spectators themselves caught in the spectacle they are contemplating, "on all the tragic scene they stare" and ask for mournful melodies. The passage between the intentional structure and the historical perspective is complete. As in so many of Borges' stories, where the dreamers are also the dreamed, the figures created into the lapis are themselves spectators of the world that has created them. They understand, quintessentially, the nature of the tragic and the mournful, and they initiate the act which reflects this understanding and by which they, as well as the lapis and the poem, are also created:

> One asks for mournful melodies;
> Accomplished fingers begin to play.
> Their eyes mid many wrinkles, their eyes,
> Their ancient, glittering eyes, are gay.

Once again in these lines we find the temporal perspective affirmed both within and outside the lapis. The wrinkles attest to the vulnerability of both the figures and the lapis to the processes of time (since we must assume that wrinkles suggest both the aging process the figures have undergone and the temporal erosion of the lapis itself). Inner and outer, the world of history and the intentional structure, are not confused but become a reflection of each other. Finally, the historical and the intentional, like the temporal and the natural, are synthesized in the gaiety with which these figures, like the characters and the actors both, perform and contemplate.

The gaiety of the figures, however, does more than relate them to the characters outside their intentional world. Gaiety in the

historical world was associated with an act of building, of creation—a futile act to some extent, but joyful too. The gaiety with
which the Chinamen play and listen to the music not only mirrors
the creativity within the historical perspective but makes of the
music the paradigmatic and irreducible act of generation. Like
Hamlet and Lear, and the actors who play them, the figures in
the lapis are starting again. And with them, too, the poem starts—
that is, with the music which is enacted by the intrusion of temporality in the lapis but which the poem itself introduces and
validates. We have in this poem an extremely complex structure,
dealing simultaneously with three intentional creations—the
music, the lapis, and the poem (and in a sense civilization itself)—
and interconnecting the acts that generate them. The connection,
once again, is given in terms of the temporality which annihilates
or at least erodes the created work but which makes the creative
act—the poem as well as the music—possible. With the start of
the music, the point of origin of the poem is located within the
poem itself. The intentional structure contains itself and also the
act by which it is generated. No song was possible in the world of
"Sailing to Byzantium." The "or" of the last stanza closed it off
to the temporal world and precluded in this sense the discovery
of its origin. Poet and protagonist, creator and creation, remained
distinct. In "Lapis Lazuli" temporality becomes not only the link
but actually the element in which these distinct worlds become to
some extent confused and interchangeable, and by which they
mirror and contain and thus complete themselves. In Keats's
"Ode," the pastness of the artistic structure informed and controlled the world of the urn. Its "history" appeared inaccessible.
But the world of the lapis, as well as the Chinamen's music and
the poem that contains them, is being constantly and historically
represented. The gaiety of creation is thus in some sense the profound subject of the poem, reflecting the repeated enactment of
the creative act within the poem and of the poem and accompanying that creation.

No conflict exists in this poem between poet and protagonist.
Indeed, even more so than in "Byzantium," the poet *is* the pro-

tagonist, creating the poem and contemplating the art-object within the poem which once again leads back into the moment of creation. But the poet is also a spectator in the poem, contemplating the historical world, the world of the lapis, and the world within the lapis, and ultimately the poem itself. The figures in the lapis create music in response to their contemplation of the world of history, but they also listen to what they create. The poet reflects this triple act of contemplation, creation, and again contemplation, but renders it more complex. He is a spectator both of history and of the lapis created in response to history; a spectator also of the figures contemplating the history which he contemplates and in which he lives. Again as in Borges, creatures and creators seem to defy the limits of their intentional universes. But the poet occupies a central and crucial position as spectator in the poem. He looks at the lapis and tells us quite pointedly that he "imagines" the figures acting as they do and the landscape looking as it does. The cracks and dents "seem" a watercourse or avalanche. It is in fact the spectator's imagination—the imagination which both contemplates and creates—that forces temporality into the poem and into the lapis by imagining movement and process in a static structure. The poetic imagination is no longer involved with the quest for stasis, for the changeless world of "Sailing to Byzantium," but instead becomes a force of mediation between two distinct and sometimes opposing worlds. The work of art becomes in fact their meeting place. We find the poet thus actively engaged not in creating a world which only a fictive protagonist could inhabit but in connecting the intentional structure and the historical process. The act of creation contained within the lapis, which mirrors the historical world twice removed from it (outside the music and outside the structure of the lapis), becomes a center which includes all other creative acts. Yet it is itself included in the act of creation of the poet, who is both creator of the poem and spectator within it, and in the act of creation within the poem, reflecting infinitely its own and history's creations.

The poem which appears at first to be self-contained thus reveals itself as a point of mediation between the intemporal and the historical. Yeats begins so often with a feeling of enclosure, of inability to break through into meaningful creation: "We are closed in, and the key is turned / On our uncertainty" (*CP*, 202). Yet he discovers, sporadically in the earlier poetry and more fully and cogently in the *Last Poems,* that the "desolation of reality" is itself the occasion for joy, the occasion to discover or create a meaningful vision of history: "Amid a place of stone, / Be secret and exult" (*CP*, 107); "Out of rock, / Out of a desolate source, / Love leaps upon its course" (*CP*, 257). Like Stevens in his later poems, Yeats affirms the capacity of poetry to sacralize profane time and to turn the gratuitous aridity of history into a landscape of imaginative redemption.

≥ STEVENS

In Wordsworth and Yeats we have seen the poetic imagination ascend, go to the edge of the abyss of consciousness, interiorize reality and reject the moment of experience. The modern imagination—already present in Yeats's later poems—turns back from the abyss and redescends into reality. It rejects the desire for absolute knowledge and through that knowledge possession of the universe and moves toward the momentary experience, the particular truth, thus giving back to reality the ontological primacy which the movement of ascension had denied it.

Stevens has by and large been seen as the great believer in the imagination. He is, but only after having become the great doubter. Only by denying the imagination its capacity for totality can he make it an instrument of the particular and perhaps chaotic richness of existence. Wordsworth ascends and almost arrives at the self-conscious creation. Yeats asserts the conscious, intentional quality of the universe he erects, then tries to break out of the tower. Stevens realizes, much earlier in his poetic career, that he must come out of that intentional universe and give back to reality its primacy.

There is, in his early poetry, a conscious withdrawal from reality which is viewed as essential to the poetic act. This withdrawal is associated with the affirmation of the imagination as the great transforming and humanizing power. Without imagination man becomes a snowman, seeing "nothing that is not there and the nothing that is." Even if confronted with a chaotic, meaningless reality the imagination imposes meaning and order on chaos, the jar in Tennessee transforms and renders habitable the natural world.

But even in the poems that assert this humanizing faculty of the imagination Stevens begins to speak about the inability of the image to reach the object and the incapacity of the imagination to truly create a world the poet can inhabit. Without imagination it is impossible to approach the "thingness" of the object. Yet this transforming power of the imagination is itself problematic. For the imagination transforms the object into something other than itself, and instead of being a mode of experience of reality it becomes an impediment, a zone of consciousness in which the mind sees nothing that is there. Stevens attempts to distinguish the rhetorical from the imaginative act, but he finds that imagination is beset by rhetoric.[1] Perhaps for this reason he rejects much earlier than Yeats the intentional universe in which his imagination tends to imprison him. But to reject the imagination and its transforming power would be to acquire the mind of the snowman, to be blinded to both the inner and outer worlds. Stevens is caught, like most modern poets, in this dialectic of consciousness and reality. Yet he achieves a certain reconciliation of these two opposing worlds. The only way the imagination may ultimately experience reality is by turning its transforming and in that measure destructive power not against reality but against itself. Thus Stevens begins to seek the metaphor that murders metaphor,[2] the image that does not attempt to name reality but instead to speak of its own incapacity to reach the "ding an sich."

1. "The relation between the poetry of experience and the poetry of rhetoric is not the same thing as the relation between the poetry of reality and that of the imagination. Experience, at least in the case of a poet of any scope, is much broader than reality" (OP, 160). The distinction here is between experience and reality, not between rhetoric and imagination.
2. Though he tells us, in "Someone Puts a Pineapple Together," to "defy / The metaphor that murders metaphor" (The Necessary Angel: Essays on Reality and the Imagination [New York: Knopf, 1951], p. 84).

By making the imagination turn against itself, the natural object is envisioned *in* the poem but placed *outside* the realm of the poem, so that the intentional structure which would normally deny the possibility of experience becomes itself the instrument of reconciliation with the outside world.

The attempted decreation of the intentional structure is accompanied by an assertion of the validity of the particular object and the particular place. The return to the particular and the assertion of the finite lead to a quest for the eternal present in the very structure of temporality, for the sudden *is* that even as it is perceived has already become a *was*. This is a poetry of failure, inevitably so because it speaks of a moment or an object that must be experienced or perceived as an absence, and of an artistic creation that can speak only of its inability to validly transform or create the world. But it is a poetry which finds its success precisely in its failure, because in its rejection of itself it ceases being an end and becomes an instrument of experience, reaching the "being" of the object in a transforming moment of awareness.

The Enclosed Space

The key symbol of this capacity for immediate perception is the light:

> The light is like a spider.
> It crawls over the water.
> It crawls over the edges of the snow.
> It crawls under your eyelids
> And spreads its webs there—
> Its two webs.   ["Tattoo"]

In "A Noiseless Patient Spider" Whitman saw the poet weaving webs of poetic creation out of himself and attaching himself, through those tenuous filaments, to reality. In Stevens' "Tattoo" the filaments are not of poetic consciousness, but of light. The light, not the poet, is like a spider. In the first stanza it weaves its webs over the water, over the snow, and under the poet's eyelids, lifting, so to speak, the film of consciousness and allowing an immediate contact with reality.

In the second stanza a further integration is carried out, between the poet and himself. The webs of his eyes move inward and are fastened to his flesh and bones "as to rafters or grass." For only the integration of the alienated "I" will permit the "eye" to see into reality, making "the axis of vision" coincident with "the axis of things."[3] In the third stanza the poet moves to an affirmation of this coincidence: "There are filaments of your eyes / On the surface of the water / And in the edges of the snow." The eyes create filaments that attach the poet to the reality of water and snow. And the light, which in the first stanza moved from reality to the self, becomes the framework in which the movement from the self to reality can be accomplished. In the act of perception the poet coincides with himself and with reality, the "eye" and the "I" are integrated through the filament and the web of light. The self is "tattooed" into reality, reality is "tattooed" on to the self.

The relation between self and world in Stevens' poetry is, however, far more problematic than it appears in "Tattoo." In the "dark" poems of *Harmonium*—"Domination of Black" and "Valley Candle"—and in "Poem with Rhythms," the consciousness of seeming undercuts the possibility of any real correspondence, and the conscious creation locks the poet in the world he has created.

"Domination of Black" opens at night. The onset of darkness is perhaps a result of the poet's withdrawal from reality through the consciousness which makes identity possible. But the consciousness which brings about darkness also brings forth the imaginative fire, through which the poet will attempt to cast light on the no longer perceptible correspondences between the object and the self.

> At night, by the fire,
> The colors of the bushes
> And of the fallen leaves,
> Repeating themselves,

3. Ralph Waldo Emerson, *Nature*.

> Turned in the room,
> Like the leaves themselves
> Turning in the wind.

The image of the room immediately establishes the enclosed space, the inner world, the intentional structure of the poetic imagination. Though the bushes and leaves repeat themselves, they repeat themselves only "by the fire," in a consciousness of similarity which undercuts all real correspondence and in a consciousness of repetition which makes impossible any true recurrence. "*Like* the leaves themselves": the seeming undercuts the capacity for being; "in the intricate evasions of as" (*CP*, 486) reality is lost. And "the color of the heavy hemlocks" comes striding; reality dies in the consciousness of imagining.

The cry of the peacocks—supposedly a stunning, strident cry—irrupts into the room. But even the sudden appearance of the peacocks in the second stanza is deprived of its immediacy by the fact that the cry is a remembered cry. The world of the poem is an inner world, a world of mirrors and echoes, of consciously intentional structures and consciously impossible repetitions of reality in the imagination. The colors of bushes and leaves turn in the room, but by the fire of the imagination, in the enclosed structure of consciousness, the colors do not become the bushes and leaves. The repetition in the room does not go farther than the conscious "like"—"the mask is strange, however like" (*CP*, 181) —the poet does not move from the imagined to the real world. There is no "escape from repetition," no "happening / In space and the self" (*CP*, 483). The domination of black, in this context, is the domination of the conscious, intentional image in its incapacity to reach the object and take hold in reality. "Set up / The rugged black, the image," Stevens says in "Prelude to Objects." But in the same poem he says "one is always seeing and feeling oneself." In "Domination of Black" he meditates on this inescapable mirroring of the self in all its attempts to reattach itself to reality. Instead of the tattoo there are the walls of the room which, as in Hölderlin's "Hälfte des Lebens," intimate the imprisonment of the conscious identity in the consciousness of its alienated self:

"In my room, the world is beyond my understanding" (*CP*, 57).

In the second stanza the peacocks are drawn into the series of associations:

> The colors of their tails
> Were like the leaves themselves
> Turning in the wind,
> In the twilight wind.

Bushes, leaves, tails are brought together by the turning of the wind and the color projected by the imagination. Yet these associations do not necessarily establish interrelations but profound alienation. The color, not the object, appears in the room. And the associations take place against the backdrop of the coloring of the imagination. In the act of imaginative perception the bushes, the leaves, and the peacocks' tails are one through the oneness of their color in the realm of the imagination. But they are one within the closed realm, the conscious structure, the alienating walls within which the blackness of the conscious image prevails. The simile undercuts the possibility of oneness, and the similarity serves only to underline the strangeness that exists between the inner and outer worlds:

> They swept over the room,
> Just as they flew from the boughs of the hemlocks
> Down to the ground.
> I heard them cry—the peacocks.

Though the remembrance of the first stanza was a conscious one, the peacocks in the second part of the second stanza become more actualized in the inner world. Now it is not the color but the peacocks themselves that sweep over the room. And it is the cry, not the memory of the cry, that the poet hears. Though the poem is in the past tense, though it is itself a past tense because it creates an experience which cannot be recreated, the duality of the cry remembered and the cry heard establishes two past tenses within the poem: the paradoxical past tense of the poetic act—inescapably a past tense because of the consciousness and interiorization involved in imaginative creation—and the past tense of the remembrance of an experience. The poet remembers an experience in the past. And he creates a new experience which is also in the past. If passage is possible from one to the other, from the cry remembered to the cry heard, can the poem become a present? Can the poetic imagination overcome the self-consciousness of the fire in an enclosed room and become an immediate expression of the self in its attachment to reality?[4]

We saw Wordsworth in "Tintern Abbey" attempting to integrate the experience and the memory of the experience into the "present" tense of the poem. Though the disjunction in "Domination of Black" is between two past tenses within the imaginative world and not between the past tense of the memory and the presence of the scene as in "Tintern Abbey," the distance between the memory and the cry suggests the inability of the imagination to represent the experience.[5]

The cry of the peacocks introduces a certain tension in the poem. It is a cry "against"—a cry standing in opposition to the interrelations of the colors. The cry against the twilight is a cry against the onset of darkness, which in this poem and through *Harmonium* in general is the darkness of the conscious image.

> Or against the leaves themselves
> Turning in the wind,
> Turning as the flames

4. It could also be argued that the peacock, for Stevens, is a figure of memory. In "Anecdote of the Prince of Peacocks," for instance, the protagonist distinguishes himself from those who forget by setting his traps "in the midst of dreams." Yeats and Seferis also see in the peacock an image of memory and thus a symbol of dissociation from reality. The peacock in Yeats's "A Man Young and Old," X, is not a "real" bird but an image in the memory, so that its cry can be only, as in "Domination of Black," a remembered cry, a cry that is "natural" only in the unnatural space of the poet's inner world. And Seferis in "Rocket" speaks of his inability to sustain a world of memory and dream, a world that can never become present.

5. Similarly Rimbaud in "Mémoire" finds himself unable to reach the flowers on the river ("ô canot immobile, oh! bras trop courts!") and recapture the experience by obliterating the past. In Whitman's "Out of the Cradle," on the other hand, the re-experienced memory obliterates all consciousness of remembrance.

>   Turned in the fire,
>   Turning as the tails of the peacocks
>   Turned in the loud fire.

Or it is a cry against an immediate reality which exists outside the poem and outside the room and which the poem cannot contain, the imagination cannot interiorize. The process here is reversed: no longer the colors turning as the leaves but the leaves themselves turning as the flames in the fire. The passage is no longer from the world to the room, from reality to the imagination, but from the conscious image to the object outside its grasp. This movement from the flames to the leaves, from the fire to the wind, begins a movement outward in the poem, one in which the poetic imagination will turn from the fire to the peacocks and attempt to walk the narrow ridge between the abyss of consciousness of the twilight and the abyss of plenitude of reality. In either case, the ultimate result may be death.

>   Out of the window,
>   I saw how the planets gathered
>   Like the leaves themselves
>   Turning in the wind.

In the third stanza an opening in the inner world appears, and a parallel opening in the poem itself. The open window functions as a potential gateway between imagination and reality, allowing the passage of the reader into the poem and the poem into the world set forth, as we will see, in "The Reader" and "The House Was Quiet and the World Was Calm." As the poetic imagination turns outward through the window, the planets gather "like the leaves themselves / Turning in the wind." The poem has moved from the past tense of a memory within another past tense to the past tense of the poem, raising the possibility of presence and integration. But though the leaves lie between the enclosed space of the room and the boundlessness of the planets, though the motion of flames and planets is similar to that of the leaves, the "like," the similarity, again underlines the difference and the space between them.

The poem thus gravitates between the interiorization and consciousness of intentionality of the poetic imagination within the room and the impossible transcendence of the planets, between the image set up "in rugged black" and the abstract image seeking totality and achieving nothingness. Wavering almost imperceptibly between the two abysses of poetry, the poem allows itself to be engulfed by a night that comes no longer from the blackness of the image but from the open window, no longer from the intentional blackness of the self-consciously creative imagination of the first stanza but from the outer darkness of which the leaves and the planets and the hemlocks are a part.

And yet, the repetition of the line and the slight change from the color of the hemlocks to the night striding "like" the color of the hemlocks tend to lead the poem back to the conscious, intentional structure it was throughout the second stanza. Through the repetition of comparisons in terms of "like," the poetic imagination tends to close the window of the third stanza and choose the blackness and the fire within.

> I felt afraid.
> And I remembered the cry of the peacocks.

To close the window is to fall into the self-conscious creation. To leave it open is to invite the night of a foreign reality to engulf the poet and the poem. In either case, "poison grows in this dark" (*CP*, 25). Related to this fear of a fall into either abyss is the memory of the cry of the peacocks—a cry against consciousness, or against reality, but also a cry of memory against the consciousness of remembrance. The poet seeks, through the poem, an identity of reality and artistic creation. As the poem goes back to the first stanza, the impossible repetitions both round it out into a consciously intentional structure and create wedges through which a passage between the work and the world might be effected. But the past tense of the remembrance within the past tense of the poem seals off these openings, closes the window, and undercuts the possibility of passage from *was* to *is*. The "dominant" of the domination of black never becomes the "tonic" of integration. It remains the unresolved black of the conscious image.

There is of course another possible reading to the poem, one which validates the function of the imagination in its dealings with reality. The bushes and leaves repeat themselves and interrelate by the fire of the imagination. The imagination colors reality, and in building relations within reality it relates to the outside world. The bushes and the leaves, repeating themselves within the realm of the imagination, are *like* the leaves themselves, like the natural object, though intentionally posed. Reality and imagination become confused—fused perhaps—in this turning and repeating. We might say that in fact they reach identity.

With the color of the heavy hemlocks the reality from the outside world once again intrudes, becoming a danger to the image and to the identity that has been established. But the imagination moves swiftly to bring the new objects—hemlocks and peacocks— into its world: the colors of their tails were "like." The imagination draws the foreign and disturbing elements of reality into the series of correspondences, and as these turn in the room and by the fire they acquire the "identity" that prevails in this enclosed space.

In the last stanza the planets appear outside the window, but again they are drawn into the similes and identities of imaginative space, until the danger of the exterior world dissolves into the comprehensive world of the imagination.

We can interpret a number of other poems in *Harmonium* in this context of imaginative interrelationships. In "The Load of Sugar-Cane," for example, one object in reality flows into the other through a series of imaginative perceptions. At the end of the poem the circle is closed, we return to the boatman of the beginning, and reality is contained in the world of the imagination.

"Valley Candle," however, also develops in the context of a domination of black:

My candle burned alone in an immense valley.
Beams of the huge night converged upon it,
Until the wind blew.
Then beams of the huge night
Converged upon its image,
Until the wind blew.

The candle burns "alone," an isolated entity in an "immense valley," a single luminous object in a world of night. But it is evident already in the title that the stress of the poem will be not on the pervading darkness or on the immensity of the valley, but on this candle, this single point of light. The candle breaks up the darkness into a multiplicity of beams, but it is the beams of the huge night that converge upon the candle, and reality that is caught in the vortex of imaginative creation. The boundless converges on the concrete, and the candle becomes essential to the darkness surrounding it. For night becomes night in relation to, in opposition to the candle, as the beams of blackness come to die in the luminous zone of the poetic consciousness. Reality is clarified and "realized" in the realm of the imagination.

Similarly in "Nuances of a Theme by Williams" the poetic consciousness wants to be totally itself in a world that is alien and perhaps inimical to its light. The poet exhorts the star to "shine alone, shine nakedly, shine like bronze . . . shine like fire, that mirrors nothing." The isolation of the star, like the "seclusion" of the candle ("Three Travelers Watch a Sunrise"), turns the poetic imagination into impenetrable bronze—a solid object that being complete in itself refuses to reflect the outer world and thus refuses to acknowledge a reality exterior to the self. The star, like the candle in the first stanza of "Valley Candle,'" suggests that its world is the only world, its space the only valid space.

The quest for completeness is true not only of the fire or the star but also of the sun itself: "The sun is seeking something bright to shine on. / The trees are wooden, the grass is yellow and thin" (CP, 157). The problem in this passage is not the star's refusal to reflect an exterior world but the sun's desire to be re-

flected in that world. If the totality of the star would be under-
mined by reflecting a reality outside itself, the sun must be
reflected in reality in order to "acquire" reality and "realize" its
light. The star was deliberately self-contained. The sun must
shine into reality. But reality is pale, impoverished, almost without
color. And thus the sun "must create its colors out of itself." The
movement which began contrary to that of the star has turned
into the same inward movement of the self that seeks completeness by a rejection of the outer world. Like the star that mirrors
nothing, the sun must be mirrored into nothing.

This intentional creation of the poetic universe is quite similar
to Yeats's creation of Byzantium. Yet imagistically the universe
Stevens erects is more fragile, more likely to be engulfed by a
reality it cannot control. Byzantium, even more than the room of
"Domination of Black," may stand changeless in a world of
change. But the candle is susceptible to the blowing of the wind.
Though Stevens begins, like Wordsworth, by believing that a
creation of reality is a discovery of reality, that creation and
revelation are simultaneous and perhaps a single act, the wind
blows, and with it the stress of the poem shifts. The candle ceases
to be a single luminous object in the night, and instead of burning
"alone" it doubles into an image of itself and loses the centrality
it held in the first part of the poem. The beams of the huge night
converge no longer on the candle but on the image of the candle,
and the image, the design, the construct usurp the centrality of
the created world. The poetic creation has superseded the act of
creation, and the beams of the night converge upon an "image-
object" that has lost the fragility and the strength of the creating
consciousness ("rubies reddened by rubies reddening," *CP*, 346),
to become a created structure in a world of change. The poem
moves away from creation as revelation and toward an intentional construct in opposition to reality.

This movement becomes clearer if seen in relation to the symbol of the wind which effects this change. The wind appears time
and again in Stevens' poems, and the key meaning in each
appearance is its incapacity to become, to *be*. It blows "among

the trees its meaningless sound" (*OP*, 44), it blows "toward an inaccessible, pure sound" (*CP*, 263). Because it is imageless, the wind is all-encompassing. But by the same token it cannot actualize itself, it cannot become a distinguishable object in reality. It never becomes the "rounding O" (*CP*, 263), the closed circle intimating completion. In "To the Roaring Wind" the wind's incapacity to become by speaking the meaningful syllable is coupled with the poet's forceful desire that it do so: "What syllable are you seeking . . . / In the distances of sleep? / Speak it." But the wind remains dissolved through a spatial reality. It cannot bring itself together into meaningful diction or a distinguishable thing, and the distances of sleep do not provide the limited space where it can find its syllable of meaning.

Like the wind that cannot actualize itself into reality, the poetic image cannot take root:

> In the way you speak
> You arrange, the thing is posed,
> What in nature merely grows.
>
> Tomorrow when the sun,
> For all your images,
> Comes up as the sun, bull fire,
> Your images will have left
> No shadow of themselves.   ["Add This to Rhetoric"]

The image is always posed metaphorically as something outside itself. Its very "nature" is to be compared to something it is not. It cannot be founded in reality, it cannot be in the mode of being of the natural object.[6] The posing of the image in this poem by Stevens implies an arrangement of nature, a fragmentation and reconstruction of reality. The imagination stylizes natural reality, "images" it, so to speak, but the images of reality are not objects-in-reality. They are immaterial entities that cannot cast shadows in the outside world. Bonnefoy places a burning torch in the gray daylight to see if it can cast a shadow, if the poetic image is indeed "truth."[7] But the poetic images in Stevens' "Add This

6. See de Man, "Intentional Structure of the Romantic Image" in *Romanticism and Consciousness*, pp. 65–77.

7. Bonnefoy, *Hier régnant désert*, "Le Visage mortel."

to Rhetoric" are as imageless as the wind, and like the wind they leave no shadow of themselves. Instead of a "correspondent breeze" connecting the self with the natural world,[8] the wind becomes in Stevens the symbol of the poet's incapacity to introduce himself in reality, to "plant" his images and truly create the world.[9]

Turning again to "Valley Candle," the beams of the night converge at first upon the candle, "until the wind blew." The blowing of the wind shifts the emphasis from the candle to the image and opens up the possibility of realization of the poetic consciousness. The image seems for a moment to have taken hold in reality and become the center of the night. The beams of the night pass from the creating consciousness to the creation of consciousness, suggesting that the artistic creation, like the jar in Tennessee, can be the center of the world, imposing meaning on a gratuitous reality. But the second blowing of the wind points to the termination of this centrality and of the power of the poetic creation to make order: "To impose is not /To discover" (*CP,* 403). The final "until" signifies the temporal destruction of this centrality and the dissolution of both image and candle in the night. Thus while in "Domination of Black" the image is ultimately enclosed in its own darkness, in "Valley Candle" it is finally engulfed by the darkness outside. In the first case it is destroyed by consciousness, in the second by reality. If the imagination in "Domination of Black" has failed to establish contact with the outside world, in "Valley Candle" it has failed to establish the proper, enclosed space of the artistic creation. "Was künstlich ist, verlangt geschlossnen Raum" (What is artistic requires an enclosed space), says Goethe's Homunculus.[10] The imageless wind has put out the candle and destroyed the image, the force incapable of realization has in turn "unrealized" the "artifice" that might have given it meaning. If the return to the past tense of the

8. Wordsworth, *The Prelude,* I, 35.
9. In "To the Roaring Wind" the wind is "vocalissimus," yet its utterance is devoid of meaning.
10. *Faust,* II, 6884.

memory in "Domination of Black" suggests the impossibility of "representation," the second introduction of "until" in "Valley Candle" suggests the irrevocable pastness of the image's power to make order. The centripetal force of the first part has turned by the second blowing of the wind into a centrifugal force that destroys the conscious creation in the dark reality which it had sought to humanize. The candle and the image of the candle are engulfed once more by the night which they had ordered and opposed.

In "Poem with Rhythms" there is a further development of the theme of the candle:

> The hand between the candle and the wall
> Grows large on the wall.

Once more the poetic imagination returns to the enclosed space of "Domination of Black." But though the image may not be able to cast a shadow, it can project the shadow of an object between the candle and the wall. The walls thus have a further function in this poem: they not only close off the artistic space from the outside world, but also provide a vertical space in which the shadows may be projected.

In the second stanza the poem jumps from the room to the outside world, on the assertion that the mind can, like the hand, be projected into reality and realize itself in real space. The image in its alienation from reality seeks to repossess reality. It has "a will to grow larger on the wall, / To grow larger and heavier and stronger than / The wall." "Poem with Rhythms" becomes a bridge between "Domination of Black" and "Valley Candle." For though the imagination needs the enclosed space in order to create, it tries to project itself beyond that enclosed space; though it needs the wall to project the shadows against it, it seeks to grow larger and heavier and stronger than the wall, outgrowing it and moving beyond it to reality. The imagination attempts to bridge the zone of nothingness between artistic space and real space.

The attempt to bridge two distinct realities occurs also in "Six Significant Landscapes." In the first landscape the old man is part of the movement of nature:

An old man sits
In the shadow of a pine tree
In China.
He sees larkspur,
Blue and white,
At the edge of the shadow,
Move in the wind.
His beard moves in the wind.
The pine tree moves in the wind.
Thus water flows
Over weeds.

The merging of the human self and the inhuman world is reminiscent of Sung paintings. The man first sees an object in nature (larkspur) move in the wind, then he responds, like the pine tree, to the movement of the wind. Responds is perhaps the wrong word. The old man is simply there, and the wind makes no distinction between the pine tree and his beard: "Thus water flows / Over weeds." We are passing in this poem, as it were, into the "natural perspective."

In the second landscape, nature (the night) is a human figure: "A pool shines, / Like a bracelet / Shaken in a dance." In both landscapes the human and the natural merge. In the third landscape, however, the relation of the human and the natural begins to break down:

I measure myself
Against a tall tree.
I find that I am much taller,
For I reach right up to the sun,
With my eye;
And I reach to the shore of the sea
With my ear.
Nevertheless, I dislike
The way the ants crawl
In and out of my shadow.

The merging of the human and the natural is no longer desirable. The protagonist begins by measuring himself *against* a tree. Through the senses he goes beyond his own particular space and reaches the sun and the sea. But his shadow points to his attach-

ment to the space in which he stands and underlines his relationship to the tree he seeks to surpass. The shadow is proof of his
materiality, and it ties him to the world he paradoxically seeks
to transcend through the senses.

We thus see in Stevens, even within a single poem, a certain
ambivalence as to the proper relationship of imagination and
reality. The "dark" poems tend to affirm the intentional creation which at the end reveals itself as entrapment and enclosure.
In "Poem with Rhythms" the imagination seeks to create images
and be its images, cause and consequence of its own genesis, "the
powerful mirror of [its] wish and will." But it can create only
within the windowless room of its inner world, distinguishing itself from the reality it seeks to penetrate or to order. Wishing to
become whole, the self ends in the ultimate alienation.

At times the mind seeks wholeness not in "dark" self-affirma-
tion but in the transparence that seems to pervade the outside
world. In "Owl's Clover" the imagination beholds itself and its
source—itself *as* its source ("Acquired transparence and beheld
itself / And beheld the source from which transparence came")—
suggesting a genesis exterior to the self which in the process of
creation becomes confused with the creating self. The poet then
becomes "the transparence of the place in which / He is and in
his poems we find peace" (*CP*, 251).

Yet transparence is often conceived as dangerously close to
annihilation. In "The Auroras of Autumn" the protagonist is
afraid of "an Arctic effulgence flaring on the frame / Of everything he is." The artistic consciousness finds itself moving inexo-
rably toward transparence and immersion in reality. The shadow
bent over the candle or the guitar, becoming the maker in the
writing of the poem or the creation of the image, discovers itself
as "frame": an infinitely fragile structure when confronted by the
sudden illumination of reality. The poet is afraid of the enclosed
world, but he is also afraid of dissolving in the plenitude of things.

This fear of exterior reality, though by no means a major
theme in Stevens, appears in yet another poem, "A Lot of People

Bathing in a Stream": "It was like passing a boundary to dive /
Into the sun-filled water." Yet to cross that boundary is infinitely
dangerous: "It was passing a boundary, floating without a head /
And naked, or almost so." The "almost so," so typical of Stevens,
saves him from dissolution but also keeps him from the experience. The end of the poem reiterates the quest for the enclosed
space and the security of a known and ordered world, where the
protagonist can move "round the rooms, which do not ever seem
to change."

These two radically different modes of arriving at a unified
self suggest not only two opposite paths of poetic creation but also
a basic disjunction between the poet's desire and the requirements
of the poetic act. Though there is in Stevens' poetry a tremendous
nostalgia for the great open spaces, for the country of the sun, the
poetic act is an act of the mind, and as such an act of enclosure.
The poetic world is thus drawn inevitably toward the enclosed
space of "Domination of Black" and the walls of "Poem with
Rhythms." Even the prisoner in "Montrachet-le-Jardin," who is
delivered by his words, finds that to create he must do so within
the cell. He seeks "deliverance." His creative act imprisons him.
And if he tries, at first, to sing "of an heroic world beyond the
cell," he immediately realizes that only the enclosed space of the
cell will make the creative act possible. "To make the cell / A
hero's world in which he is the hero" indicates the framework
necessary for the poetic act. Consciousness alienates and imprisons.
But the deliverance from consciousness through an act of consciousness itself requires the boundaries of that conscious world.
The cell in fact becomes the informing image in much of modern
poetry. Wordsworth's Mary Queen of Scots called for the enclosed space that would fit her "altered state." But Wordsworth
never sought to create within the cell. Stevens finds that the creative act imposes a spatial limitation which denies, precisely, the
poet's attempt to experience reality. The poetic creation involves
so often a tragic vision not because it does not achieve what it sets
out to achieve, but because in its very essence it is at odds with
the world it has not created. Stevens begins by believing in the

power of the imagination to order reality and create "its" world out of "the" world: "Imagination is the will of things" (*CP*, 84). He seeks to cleanse reality of its chaos by imaginatively recreating it. Yet to experience reality and to give meaning and order to reality are two different and opposing acts, and the poems that seek this creation of order are ultimately anecdotes, preludes, asides, extracts, notes, prologues, nuances, metaphors that turn against the symbol that creates it.

The Ordered World

In "Anecdote of the Jar," the jar in Tennessee imposes itself on reality, *making* the slovenly wilderness become ordered around it. It draws reality into its ordered realm, it takes "dominion" in the natural world. But unlike everything else in Tennessee, it cannot bring the world into being, it cannot "give of bird or bush." Like the man with the blue guitar, who "cannot bring a world quite round," the poet can only fragment and reconstruct reality, posing intentionally, metaphorically, "what in nature merely grows" (*CP*, 198).

In "The Idea of Order at Key West" Stevens explores further this problem of the relation of art and nature. The artistic construct in this poem is not a specific object with a definable form. It is a song whose form is not given in the poem, whose essence it is to be shaped by the reality it "poematizes." The song is thus more immediate, more at one with the singer, more the act itself of creation than the creation isolated from the act that brought it into being. "She sang beyond the genius of the sea." Stevens begins time and again with a desire to order reality into a world he can inhabit. But he cannot bring himself to deny the validity of the unordered reality, "untouched / By trope or deviation" (*CP*, 471). The "genius" of reality lies in its elusiveness, in its refusal to be mastered by the world of art. Because the song is more the expression of the singer than the conscious creation of the poet, it achieves in this poem a certain union with reality. The girl sings of the sea, beyond the sea, and the song and the sea merge and yet remain distinct from each other. That the song suggests music, which is apprehended more immediately through the sense, also helps to establish this relationship. The water is never "formed" in the song or by the song. It remains itself, its sound mingling with and informing the song: "The sea was not a mask. No more was she." Neither is "like." They both are.

But the "inhuman" sound of the "veritable ocean" is humanized by the poetic creation:

> It may be that in all her phrases stirred
> The grinding water and the gasping wind;
> But it was she and not the sea we heard.

Though the singer may be one with the song, though she may sing about reality, she does not sing reality itself. Between the song and the sea lies the identity of the maker, the image that is not the object, the word that cannot be. If the song were reality, it would be "a summer sound / Repeated in a summer without end." But it is "a little different from reality" (*CP,* 344), endowing with meaning "the meaningless plungings of water and the wind." The girl sings "beyond the genius of the sea," and beyond the ending of her song the sea is portioned out. But as the voice of the poet in the poem withdraws from the song, the virtual ordering of reality becomes an unfulfilled desire. There never was another world for the singer of the song. But the writer of the poem, within the poem itself, sees the song end.

Thus Stevens moves in "Key West" from an affirmation of poetry's capacity to become one with reality, simultaneously revealing and creating it, to a realization that the act of creation entails a structuring and defining of reality that separates the poem from the real. The progress of the poem lies in this deepening awareness of its distance from the song. The song fading at the end leaves "ghostlier demarcations, keener sounds," but also a "rage for order" that is not assuaged.

The same movement of attempted integration and ultimate withdrawal occurs in "The Man with the Blue Guitar." As in "Key West," the poet wishes to integrate reality to his imaginative

creation of reality, "a tune upon the blue guitar / Of things
exactly as they are." That tune, like the song of the girl, would
create a "place" in reality where the poet would be totally himself and totally at one with the world. But when the poet plays a
tune on the guitar, it is always a tune that makes reality "different," a creation that distorts the object and renders impossible the
experience of an untouched world. The tune poses the object, but
the object itself closes up in an impenetrable objectivity. "A tune
beyond us as we are, / Yet nothing changed by the blue guitar"
would require the impossible coincidence of imagination and
reality, and it would constitute the foundation of the place of
being. But "things as they are / Are changed upon the blue
guitar." The poet cannot bring a world into existence, he can
only "patch" together the fragments of a reality he has interior-
ized. The "buzzing of the blue guitar" is not quite the "buzzing
of flies in autumn air," and in fact the composing of the guitar
destroys the world that it has "recomposed": "Things as they are
have been destroyed." For how does the poet name the reality of
the real when he can only add adjectives to nouns and make
subtle distinctions between object and attribute? To call the sun
good, merciful, immaculate is to reveal the poet's inability to say
anything significant about reality. Description of the real becomes
detachment from the real. The human becomes the alien in a
place that stands "remote" from all his efforts to possess it.

The sense of remoteness is central to Stevens' concept of the
relation of self and world. In "The Blue Guitar" description increases remoteness and unreality and makes the sense of "foreignness" of the world and the self more acute. "The pale intrusions
into blue / Are corrupting pallors," and the adjectives, like the
conscious creations, introduce the particular coloring of the imagination into the objects the poet wishes to describe and humanize:

> Throw away the lights, the definitions,
> And say of what you see in the dark
>
> That it is this or that it is that,
> But do not use the rotted names.

There is a tendency in every poet who feels the limitations of language as keenly as Stevens does to reduce poetry to silence, to reject poetry because it cannot approximate reality. Hölderlin goes mad. Rimbaud stops writing. Stevens begins with a belief in the power of the imagination to transform a chaotic reality into a habitable world, yet he doubts the capacity of the imagination to impose order without destroying reality, to name things in their essence without enveloping them in opacity. The poet seeks transparence and is left with the rugged black of the image. He seeks a meaningful world and is left with a jar that cannot give of bird or bush. "The lion in the lute" becomes "the lion locked in stone." In the beginning of the poem Stevens suggests that the world is "flat and bare," that the imagination has to create its own world and fill the heavens emptied by the death of the gods. But the world thus created is not valid for the self that has created it, and Stevens rejects the transformations of the guitar because they cannot approximate the world he does not wish to reject. "There is no place, / Here, for the lark fixed in the mind." Because the conscious creation cannot become a "rhapsody of things as they are," Stevens relegates the poem to a momentary place, a divertimento which is a diversion from reality: "The moments when we choose to play / The imagined pine, the imagined jay." The double meaning of the word "play"—suggesting both music and diversion—points to the poet's rejection of his poem as "reality." For the temporal and spatial duration of the poem there is "an absence in reality," but one which, Stevens suggests, may be "an absence for the poem" in which reality is not denied but validated. We see here a foreshadowing of the later poetry, where the imagination turning upon itself will effect a return to the natural world.

But "The Blue Guitar" is still a poem *of the mind,* "in the act of finding / What will suffice" (*CP,* 239). What would suffice, as for Yeats, would be an imagination that would be cause and consequence of itself, creating and inhabiting the world. The mind "cannot be half earth, half mind; half sun, / Half thinking; until the mind has been satisfied . . ." (*CP,* 257). The mind cannot be satisfied unless it possesses reality, unless earth and sun are also part of itself. To know that there is a reality outside, beyond the realm of its control, is to know that all thought must be dualistic and representational. This is why Yeats seeks out "images that yet / Fresh images beget,"[11] and Stevens has the imagination construct its own stage and enact its quest for "the book of reconciliation" (*CP*, 345). Both efforts fail because the mind interiorizes the reality of a fragmented and reconstructed world. Unable to inhabit a reality it has not created, and equally unable to believe in a world it has created out of itself, "it can never be satisfied, the mind, never" (*CP*, 247). Only a dual act of possession and participation could achieve "what" would to the mind suffice. The "what" is an undetermined moment or place, but more than a moment or a place it would have to comprise the universe and the mind that perceives and reconstructs it.

There are a few instances in Stevens' poetry in which he attempts to reach such a dual act, creating and becoming one with his world, making the poem and the world coincide:

> All night I sat reading a book,
> Sat reading as if in a book
> Of sombre pages.

As do some early poems of *Harmonium*, "The Reader" develops against the background of darkness, in which the reader, like the poet, must create his own light. In the first stanza the reader goes from the reading *of* a book to reading himself *into* a book-like world. The simile of the second line—"as if"—belies the statement of the first line as to the reality of the book. But this denial of the reality of the book (and thus of the poem) leads to an assertion of the reality of the world and to a passage of the reader into that world. In pivoting on the structure of language the poem passes from the book to a denial of the book and the introduction of the book into the reality of the universe. Yet reality itself bears the traces of the book: it is divided into "sombre pages," suggesting that it, too, is an intentional structure whose intentionality is beyond the reader's understanding.

11. "Byzantium."

"No lamp was burning as I read." The reader is no longer the creator of the universe but the perceiver of it, perceiving the book opening up into a larger reality and the autumn world falling into the coldness of winter. The passage from the book to the world, from the intentional structure to the reality that eludes control, is marked by a falling back into coldness, by a passage from the fruition of autumn to the winter wasteland. The reader has gone from the intentional structure of the book or poem into the supposedly intentional structure— "as if"—of the universe. "The sombre pages bore no print / Except the trace of burning stars / In the frosty heaven." The simile of the world as a book is carried over into the last stanza. The sombre pages intimate that the world, like the book, is a text that man can read. But the sombre quality of the pages, and particularly the lack of print, suggest the absence of signs through which the book of reality might be read. Through the symbols of language the reader penetrates the meaning of a book or poem. But the sombre pages remain sombre and cold because the objects in reality, if they are signs, remain closed within themselves, refusing to become print and yield to us their significance. Hölderlin's definition of man as a sign deprived of significance ("Ein Zeichen sind wir, deutungslos")[12] is ultimately the knowledge the reader gains of the universe he seeks to read. The "as if" of the first stanza, the absence of a lamp, and finally the absence of print suggest that the world may be read, perhaps, as a book, but that it ultimately eludes the reader's understanding.

In "The Reader" the protagonist passes into the book and into the world. In "The House Was Quiet and the World Was Calm" he passes into the book and into the poem itself:

> The house was quiet and the world was calm.
> The reader became the book; and summer night
>
> Was like the conscious being of the book.
> The house was quiet and the world was calm.

Abruptly in the second line the oneness of reader and book is

12. "Mnemosyne," second version.

proclaimed. Because the reader becomes one with the book and with the symbolic world he seeks to understand, the book becomes a "conscious being" in a world that refuses to yield its symbolic value. Even the similarity of the adjectives "quiet" and "calm," applied to the house (the enclosed space) and the world (natural reality), suggests that a certain connection between the intentional structure and the outside world has been established. This unspoken coincidence, in the first two couplets, of two worlds outside the reader—the book and summer night—makes possible the free movement of the reader from one to the other and the sudden statement "the reader became the book." In this oneness of the house and the world, the book and summer night, the artistic structure ceases being an intentional construct to become a "conscious being" in a world where consciousness would normally be rejected. The book, the conscious creation, the finished construct, "becomes," finding its essence in summer night. And the reader who is both reader of the book and reader of the summer night suddenly enters the world of reality that had remained closed to him in "The Reader." "The words were spoken as if there was no book." The words cease being metaphors posed outside themselves and become signs that reveal the significance of the summer night. The book (the actual book) and the book of the world coincide in the beginning of this poem. And the reader too (the reader of the poem and the reader in the poem) becomes a "conscious being" in a world where words and objects have coincided.

But the "except" of the third couplet introduces the problem of creation:

> The words were spoken as if there was no book,
> Except that the reader leaned above the page.

The reader leans above the page, a little like the man with the blue guitar, in a gesture of expectancy. And the expectation, as in "The Blue Guitar," is to arrive at the coincidence of the book and the world. If the book could become a "conscious being" in summer night, if summer night could become "a perfection of thought," then the dichotomy of thought and being would no longer inform every human act. The progression of the poem in this sense belies the abrupt statement of the second line. For the trend of the poem will be to achieve the coincidence it claims to have achieved in the beginning, to arrive at "the access of perfection to the page." The access of perfection to the page, in this sense, depends on the reader reading the poem backward and passing from the leaning action which indicates distance into the "conscious being" of the beginning in which distance has been obliterated. The conscious being of the book in summer night and the perfection of thought must become one so that the reader can have access to the perfection of the page, so that he can read, in a single act, the book and the world.

In the last two couplets the perfection of the beginning of the poem is recaptured:

> And the world was calm. The truth in a calm world,
> In which there is no other meaning, itself

> Is calm, itself is summer and night, itself
> Is the reader leaning late and reading there.

The first "calm" is a predicate adjective that describes the world and distances the poem from the world. The construction of the last couplet turns the second "calm" into a predicate noun. The world is calm, but like the predicate nouns "summer" and "night," it is also *the calm*. The house is quiet, but it is also *the quiet,* and "the quiet was part of the meaning, part of the mind." In this passage from predicate adjective to predicate noun there is a movement within the poem toward the access of perfection to the page. The verb "to be" links two subjects (*"the truth* is calm" and *"the calm* is truth") and equals them (*"the truth* is *the calm"*), if not grammatically at least poetically into a single reality. The reader leaning above the page may read backward or forward, the end of the poem has recaptured the perfection of the beginning. And the reader of the poem becomes the reader in the poem. In the artistic structure within the artistic structure the hypothetical door is flung open. In the space of the poem, the poem and the world have coincided.

Yet the few poems that offer a coincidence of the book and the world—"The Reader," "The House Was Quiet," "The Poem that Took the Place of a Mountain," and "Three Travelers Watch a Sunrise"—do so in terms of pastness, and darkness, and enclosure. In these poems that speak of union rather than alienation, we encounter the same enclosed space, the same rugged black, the same irrevocable pastness. In coming together, the book and the world have not "realized" but fictionalized each other. Only if reality becomes fictional can the fiction of the book become real. In all these poems reality has been caught within the pages of a book, enclosed in a structure inimical to the very concept of reality as Stevens conceives it. There is no experience, there is only an attempt at understanding and possession which ultimately does not suffice.

In "The Poem that Took the Place of a Mountain" the past tense once more suggests that if an experience has occurred, the mountain has recovered its place in reality, that the poem is a poem *about*. The protagonist, as in "The Reader," establishes a close relation to the poem he is reading. But unlike the protagonist of "The Reader," he does not pass into the poem. He remembers, instead, "how he had recomposed the pines." Reality has been deliberately fragmented and recomposed, as in Baudelaire's "Paysage," but the "success" of the poem does not endure. To be complete the poet has to understand and participate in reality. He must possess reality through the intelligence and participate in it through the senses. But the completion of the self and of reality must remain unexplained, for to explain is to fragment and interiorize. The protagonist recomposes the natural scene, seeking the proper outlook. But he is hemmed in by the past tense of the poem and the conditional tense of the "achieved" completeness. The poem that *took* the place of a mountain is precisely a poem that has returned to its poetic structure.

This consciousness of structure becomes particularly significant in "Three Travelers Watch a Sunrise." The play opens with the

shine of a lantern: "All you need, / To find poetry, / Is to look
for it with a lantern." The lantern lights the dark, it implies a
controlled recomposing of reality which the sun rising at the end
will destroy. The controlled re-creation is referred to in the play
as "seclusion": "There is a seclusion of porcelain / That humanity never invades." The artistic structure is detached from human
concerns. It is eternal and above history. Seclusion, detachment,
intentionality: the three themes are closely interwoven in Stevens.
The intentional structure creates an enclosed space, a space of
seclusion, and necessitates a detachment from exterior reality.
This detachment becomes evident in the illustration of the second
Chinese:

> This candle is the sun;
> This bottle is earth:
> It is an illustration
> Used by generations of hermits.
> The point of difference from reality
> Is this:
> That, in this illustration,
> The earth remains of one color—
> It remains red,
> It remains what it is.
> But when the sun shines on the earth,
> In reality
> It does not shine on a thing that remains
> What it was yesterday.
> The sun rises
> On whatever the earth happens to be.

The illustration operates in the seclusion of the candle. Being an
intentional construct, like the metaphor it remains static, it
cannot change with the changing earth. The earth is never what
it was, but for the man on the dump today's azaleas and so on
are tomorrow's azaleas and so on. The future emerges out of the
past, and there is no break, no "freshness of poetry by the sea"
(*OP*, 37).

The candle and the sun are thus distinguished in this play in
terms of seclusion and change. The candle remains what it was

in a recomposed world that has not changed either. The sun comes up on a different world each time, a world without past and without future. But the third Chinese suggests that there may be another meaning to "seclusion," through which the candle and the sun might be brought together. The candle sometimes shines "for the beauty of shining":

> That is the seclusion of sunrise
> Before it shines on any house.

Seclusion is seen here as virtuality, the light of the candle or the sun *before* it rises on reality, *before* it casts light on either world.

The second Chinese does not agree. The candle's seclusion, even if the light is only virtual, still casts the same light on a changeless world:

> What the court saw was always of the same color,
> And well shaped,
> And seen in a clear light.

The court never saw "the flawed jars, / The weak colors, / The contorted glass," the flaw in the structure that would indicate the intrusion of reality into the world of art. As in the poetry of his later years, Stevens is here suggesting that only the flaw in the artistic construct can intimate a reality beyond the confines of its intentional world. But in this play he seeks a different resolution. Instead of destroying the artistic structure, he introduces an artistic structure within another artistic structure, so that the framework within the framework may "realize" the fictitiousness of the secluded world. The second Chinese calls this "the invasion of humanity":

> If it be supposed that we are three figures
> Painted on porcelain
> As we sit here,
> That we are painted on this very bottle . . .

The characters in the play introduce themselves into another work of art within the play, they become figures on the porcelain jar. And the lady in the ballad that one of the Chinese will sing a little later becomes the lady in the play. The movement back and forth from one artistic structure into the other suggests that passage might also be possible between the poem and the world. If the characters in an artistic frame can step out into the "reality" of another artistic frame, as they do in Robbe-Grillet's *Dans le labyrinthe*, then the characters in the play can step out into the larger structure of the world. Whether this process "realizes" the artistic creation or "fictionalizes" the world into an artistic structure is not made clear in "Three Travelers Watch a Sunrise." For Borges the device so common to fantastic literature makes the world fiction so that two alien realities may coincide: "These inversions suggest that if the characters of a fictional work can be readers or spectators, we, its readers or spectators, can be fictitious."[13] But Stevens still tries to direct the poem or the play into reality. Particularly in the case of the ballad, the characters in the intentional structure of the ballad are "realized" into the intentional structure of the play: "The young gentleman of the ballad," says the first Chinese, surprised to see him on the stage of the play. The question is whether the characters in the play can be similarly "realized" into reality, whether the irruption of the real world into the flawed porcelain can make an interchange possible. Then the "shadow hunched / Above the arrowy, still strings" would become both *maker* and *made*.

There is certainly a movement to eliminate the dividing line between the two artistic structures. The ballad shows the creation influenced by the process of creating: "And can you tell how it will end?" And finally the consciousness of the framework leads to a destruction of the framework and a merging of two structures: "And the end of the ballad. / Take away the bushes." The framework of the ballad has been destroyed, and the characters in the ballad have become characters in the play. Two distinct realities seem to have come together. And yet, the man that has gone from the ballad to the play cannot endure two "realities," or the consciousness of fiction, and hangs himself. The ballad and the play are fictional entities, and the "seclusion of porcelain," the "seclusion of sunrise" are precisely secluded realities, intentional structures.

13. Borges, *Labyrinths,* p. 196.

> The candle of the sun
> Will shine soon
> On this hermit earth.
> > [*indicating the bottle*]
> It will shine soon
> Upon the trees,
> And find a new thing
> > [*indicating the body*]
> Painted on this porcelain,
> > [*indicating the trees*]
> But not on this.
> > [*indicating the bottle*]

The bottle, in the beginning of the play, was used to signify earth. The body of the man will be painted on the artistic structure, but not on reality. Paradoxically the bottle "signifies" what cannot be signified, it is used to illustrate a reality that will reject illustrations.

> And as the red of the sun
> Is one thing to me
> And one thing to another,
> So it is the green of one tree
> And the green of another,
> Without which it would all be black.
> Sunrise is multiplied,
> Like the earth on which it shines,
> By the eyes that open on it,
> Even dead eyes,
> As red is multiplied by the leaves of trees.

Were it not for the difference of red and green and the difference in perception, "it would all be black," the world would be the world of "Domination of Black" or "Valley Candle." But the seclusion of the candle is finally rejected in this play. Instead of the enclosed space, the ordered world, we have an acceptance of multiplicity and a chaotic reality. Real sunshine is not secluded, it has no single form, it cannot be structured. It shines differently for each person, and only in chaotic multiplicity can it retain its "unsecluded" quality. "Sunrise is multiplied," and only this acceptance of chaotic richness can overcome the domination of black. In Yeats multiplicity belonged to "the mirror-scalèd ser-

pent,"[14] it was the consequence of man's desire for knowledge
and his fragmentation of the world he sought to possess. In
Stevens multiplicity is beyond all knowledge and possession. It
suggests the richness of reality, and in its rejection of "ideas of
order" it makes possible the poet's attachment to the particular
object in a multiple world.

The Rejection of Metaphor

Multiplicity and particularity must still be achieved through
the poetic word. In "By Broad Potomac's Shore" Whitman offers
a prayer to reality, for reality, asking that the poetic creation be
infused with a reality outside itself. Stevens, too, speaks of "conceiving words, / As the night conceives the sea-sounds in silence"
(CP, 86). The use of the same verb for the poetic creation and
for the natural process suggests that the imaginative conception
may indeed be an organic act, that the words may be conceived
as epiphanic manifestations rather than conscious creations. But
words conceived in the mode of being of the natural object are
conceived "in silence." The attempted creation of reality ends in
a silencing of the word in face of a reality it cannot name, order,
or "conceive." Stevens wants to jump the zone of consciousness,
passing "from that which was conceived to that / Which was
realized" (CP, 354), turning the individual act of consciousness
into a universal act of reality. "Not the symbol but that for which
the symbol stands" (CP, 238), the poetic creation would be a
creation of reality. But to achieve this coincidence the poet would
have to create with "letters of rock and water, words / Of the
visible elements and of ours" (CP, 232).

Time and again Stevens contends that such creation is possible: "the world / Goes round in the climates of the mind / And
bears its floraisons of imagery" (OP, 102). The images here are
no longer alienating entities, springing from consciousness and
stylizing reality. They are emerging as naturally as the flower, and
the alien world that comes into contact with the mind "bears" the

14. "Supernatural Songs," II.

flowers that bespeak the union of both. The mind, in fact, is no longer subject to moods but to climates: mental processes have become "naturalized."

If words and images are objects-in-reality, then the natural objects no longer close their meaning within themselves. The word-thing is "a sign of meaning in the meaningless" (*CP*, 529), a symbol that is not a stylization of reality but a revelation of it— "the presence of the intelligible / In that which is created as its symbol" (*CP*, 529). Creation is revelation, and the image does not usurp reality but lays bare the essence of the real: "as in images we awake, / Within the very object that we seek, / Participants of its being" (*CP*, 463). Consciousness and reality would seem to merge in this reading of the image as a pathway into the object.

But Stevens begins to meditate, even before "The Blue Guitar," on the incapacity of the word, the image, the poem, to name the object in its essence or capture it in its immediacy. That "it is a world of words to the end of it" (*CP*, 345) is the problem rather than the solution: "The words of things entangle and confuse. / The plum survives its poems" (*CP*, 41). In "Extracts from Addresses to the Academy of Fine Ideas" he compares "the silent rose of the sun" with "this paper, this dust." To the natural flower he opposes the rose of paper, the rose of words on paper, and then goes on to suggest that the sun, the sky, the natural world, are rendered artificial through the written word. The natural rose is a "silent rose," beyond the power of the word to alter or experience it. It lives "in its smell," complete in itself, and defies the poet to penetrate the circle of perfection of its being. The metaphor, on the other hand, is an artifice that cannot take hold in reality. It is "never the thing but the version of the thing" (*CP*, 332), never the immediate object but the conscious image that the natural world rejects. Each version is a projection a little different from reality and ultimately a diversion from the object it projects. Instead of finding in metaphor a generation of reality, the poet sees "metaphor as degeneration" (*CP*, 444), always altering the object and undermining the possible experience.

In "The Motive for Metaphor," for example, the poet refuses to arrive at a metaphor and remains with the motive of a metaphor still unformed. The poem opens with the blowing of the wind, blowing words without meaning in a reality itself devoid of meaning. In the half-deadness of autumn and the half-colors of spring, happiness and a single bird seem to foreshadow "Of Mere Being." But this is no golden, bronzed decor. An obscure moon lights an obscure world, suggesting the incapacity of the object to be expressed and to become itself in a passage from silence to speech. Yet to express things, to light the obscure world of reality, the metaphor must usurp the "thingness" of the object, casting it into a shape that is not its own. Stevens stops short of the metaphor here and ends the poem on the dominant X. X is the enigma of reality not contained in metaphor, and the "dominant" quality of X underlines the presence of this enigma by implying, beyond the idea of domination, a sense of something unresolved. The motive rather than the metaphor, the enigmatic X rather than the clarified reality, become the valid subjects of poetry. The way toward decreation of the poem and the sudden experience of reality begin with this acceptance of motive over metaphor, the enigma over the resolution. "How many poems he denied himself / In his observant progress, lesser things / Than the relentless contact he desired" (*CP*, 34). Crispin never arrives at the relentless contact, but by rejecting the total reconstruction of reality Stevens attempts to reach the unmediated experience.

The rejection of totality begins, as we have seen, by a rejection of metaphor. In "Metaphors of a Magnifico"

> Twenty men crossing a bridge,
> Into a village,
> Are twenty men crossing twenty bridges,
> Into twenty villages,
> Or one man
> Crossing a single bridge into a village.

The individual consciousnesses of twenty men make reality different for each, and the single bridge and village turn into twenty bridges and villages. Or else there is a singleness of perception by

which the twenty men become one man crossing the bridge into
the village. The assumption of sameness or difference, of course,
takes place in the mind of the perceiver, who refuses to make a
choice. "This is old song / That will not declare itself." The song
introduced into the poem would create a framework within
the framework, except that the song does not declare itself, it is
not enacted. The poet's quest is to go beyond the various metaphors to the origin of song. But the song remains silent, and in a
sense uncreated.

> Twenty men crossing a bridge,
> Into a village,
> Are
> Twenty men crossing a bridge
> Into a village.

Stevens rejects here the infinite possibilities of metaphor, two of
which he had presented in the first stanza—that the twenty men
were twenty men crossing twenty bridges into twenty villages, or
one man crossing a bridge into a village. Here the verb "to be"
links two equal statements—twenty men crossing a bridge into a
village are twenty men crossing a bridge into a village—suggesting
that there is no possible metaphor to express the variations of
reality. The second stanza thus rejects even the simple correlations
of the first and makes the poem move toward the simplicity and
silence of song. The old song will not declare itself, it is as silent
as the sounds of reality. In rejecting the metaphoric posing of the
object or even the variations of the first stanza, the second stanza
begins to adopt the undeclared quality of the song and leads the
poem to decreate itself. To reach reality, it has to silence itself.
"That will not declare itself / Yet is certain as meaning": the
untold reality is meaningful precisely because it is untold. It is
"certain" because it is not ordered by the distinctive individual
consciousness which makes poetry possible. Poetry, in this sense,
is always a destructive force, a force that re-creates and destroys
the real: "She searched / The touch of springs, / And found /
Concealed imaginings" (*CP*, 90). There is no contact, only
divergings from reality. Later Stevens will seek the immediate

aspect of objects which makes "imaginings of them lesser things" (*CP*, 430). In "Metaphors of a Magnifico" the essential meaning of reality and the certainty of meaning of the unsung song elude thought: "Of what was it I was thinking? / So the meaning escapes."

In "The Idea of Order at Key West" Stevens contends that the song masters reality even after it ends. In "Metaphors of a Magnifico" the unsung song attracts the poet to reality. In "Key West" the song is alluded to in the poem but never introduced verbally into its structure. In "Metaphors of a Magnifico" it is not clear whether the poem *is* the song, whether the partial refrain is an irruption of the song into the poem or a destruction of the poem in commenting on the song. In rejecting metaphor, in approximating the simplicity of song, the poem slowly becomes the song that is undeclared. The comments on the song are comments on itself: "This is old song . . . / That will not declare itself / Yet is certain as meaning." Finally, the comment on the song takes off from the third stanza, and the repetition of the white wall and the fruit trees in the apparently formless refrain suggests that the poem, in the measure in which it has become the song, is open-ended. The poet cannot recollect the experience or round it off into the perfect structure of "Domination of Black." But precisely because the poem is "imperfect," because it fades into the undeclared song and rejects the posing of metaphor, it draws closer to reality. The meaning of the scene escapes and, as it does, the poem seems to melt into the scene. The poet pursues the meaning into the last refrain, but the unfinished sentences taken from the third stanza suggest an increasing distance between meaning and reality. As the meaning eludes the poem, the poem paradoxically moves closer to the certainty of reality. The rejection of metaphor, the irruption of song—the refrain that breaks the continuity—and finally the sense of open-endedness and the deliberate diffusion of the song in space turn the poem itself into a bridge leading into the reality of white walls and fruit trees.

In "Of the Surface of Things" the subject of the poem is again the impossibility of the enactment of song within the poem:

> In my room, the world is beyond my understanding;
> But when I walk I see that it consists of three or four
>   hills and a cloud.

The first line establishes the dichotomy between the inner enclosed space and the outside world. In undercutting that space, the protagonist moves outward and begins to see.

In the second stanza he returns to a simile he had written about that outside world—"The spring is like a belle undressing" —and implicitly rejects the simile. What is particularly interesting about this poem is how much is implied, successfully, about the protagonist's inability to say anything about reality. The poem rejects what the poet has written. The deliberately trite simile seems at the same time to spread out into the poem and invalidate it, and to become the point at which the poem rejects itself.

The third stanza consists of three separate statements in which reality is woven into a song that, as in "Key West," is never sung, or, as in "Metaphors of a Magnifico," does not declare itself.

A similar use of song occurs in "Country Words": "It was an old rebellious song, / An edge of song that never clears." Again the poet cannot reach the song, as he cannot reach reality. The song is "rebellious" because, like the objects in reality, it does not yield to us its meaning. It is an edge of song, a partial creation that does not reveal its structure, that eludes, rather, the conscious structuring of the imagination. Country words are not enough to turn poetry into song.

Again in "Poem Written at Morning" the poetic metaphors are the divisive elements between the poet and reality. Through the metaphor the object is posed into "this" or "that"—always into something that violates its "thingness." "It is this or that / And it is not. / By metaphor you paint / A thing." The painting of metaphor is ultimately a faking of reality, not a valid means of experiencing it: "The strawberries once in the Apennines . . . / They seem a little painted, now. / The mountains are scratched and used, clear fakes" (CP, 226).

Stevens returns to this idea in "The Common Life": "The paper is whiter / For these black lines." In a first reading, reality is made more "acute" by the poetic image. But if the paper is reality, the black lines fail to impose a pattern, and instead make the blank paper glare in defiance. Whiteness and colorlessness finally engulf the poetic imagination. And the ink remains to make the unordered reality glare against the imposed pattern. "The paper is whiter," but "the men have no shadows / And the women have only one side." The creative act does not give of bird or bush, and the metaphoric posing is as one dimensional as a painting by Seurat. Without shadow and without volume, the poetic image serves only to make more "acute" its unreality and to allow the whiteness of the paper to cover the possible design.

This preoccupation with the image as lifeless painting is discussed further in "So-And-So Reclining on Her Couch." There is a sense of anonymity in the title, or perhaps a sense of the unimportance, or even the impossibility, of identity. So-And-So is anybody, and what is important is that it does not matter who it is. She is anybody, but she cannot become somebody, for as the poem progresses it is evident that she cannot "become."

> On her side, reclining on her elbow.
> This mechanism, this apparition,
> Suppose we call it Projection A.

It is not certain at what point the reader realizes that the object in question is a sculpture (though the argument could also be made that it is a painting). But there is from the first line a sense of something contrived, forced into a pose. Perhaps because the pose is so unnatural it may be taken as a symbol of the posing of metaphor. The work of art is a "mechanism" lacking the vital, organic aspects of reality. It is a projection in a series of projections. If the work of art is a conscious structure "vitally deprived" of reality, the consciousness of intentionality is carried further by the poet who speaks of this work in terms of a series of projections. The cold detachment of the sculpture is matched by the cold detachment of the poet. In speaking of art, the poem speaks about itself, and Projections A, B, C, are ways in which it attacks its own "mechanism," its own intentional posing. Though there is a feeling of nonchalance in the first stanza—"suppose we call it. . ."—the seriousness of the poet's rejection of the intentional structure is unquestionable.

> She floats in air at the level of
> The eye, completely anonymous,
> Born, as she was, at twenty-one,
>
> Without lineage or language, only
> The curving of her hip, as motionless gesture.

That she floats in air underlines her rootlessness in reality, the fact that she was never conceived naturally but created intentionally, mechanically, "at twenty-one." The intentional construct denies natural processes. The "birth" of the figure is an *ex-nihilo* conception, "anonymous" because she has no identity other than the artist's intention. Identity and intention, for the creator as well as the creation, are mutually exclusive. The creator seeks to become himself through his creation and finds that he has created an image of himself. And the creation is "without lineage or language," without past or future, and without means of expression. Raised out of the temporal, like the bird of Byzantium it cannot sing into reality, and it cannot be. The "motionless gesture" suggests a movement forever about to take place, caught like Keats's urn in the deadening eternity of its pose. The pose, like the metaphor, is incapable of thrusting itself into the "now" of reality.

> If just above her head there hung,
> Suspended in air, the slightest crown
> Of Gothic prong and practick bright,
>
> The suspension, as in solid space,
> The suspending hand withdrawn, would be
> An invisible gesture. Let this be called
>
> Projection B.

In the first three stanzas the sculpture was presented in its anonymity and its inability to become. Here the "invisible gesture" introduces into the sculpture, and consequently into the poem, the process of creation. The artist hypothetically suspends "the slightest crown." But the "invisible gesture" inevitably becomes the "motionless gesture" of Projection A, and Projection B shares with Projection A the inability to actualize itself in "solid space." "The suspending hand [is] withdrawn," and the creation closes in upon itself.

There is, however, a progression from projection to projection. In Projection A the sculpture was anonymous, the artist ostensibly absent. In Projection B the artist introduces himself into the sculpture and withdraws, underlining the intentional aspect of his creation. In Projection C we are told that the woman in the sculpture "is half who made her."

> She is half who made her.
> This is the final Projection, C.

The artist, deliberately absent in Projection A (since the woman was anonymous), entering and withdrawing in Projection B, becomes the definite creator in Projection C. The sculpture is an intentional structure, created in an act of consciousness, not of reality. It is not reality that the artist reveals in his creation, but himself. Yet he is also denied access to it. Precisely because he is present in it, because it is an image of himself, it lacks the reality of what has not been intentionally created. When he enters, as in Projection B, to add an invisible gesture, it is only to underline its intentional quality. He is caught, like the sculpture, between "the thing as idea and / The idea as thing," between the conceptualization of reality inherent in artistic creation and the impossible actualization of an intentional construct. The act of consciousness never becomes an act of reality, and from the anonymity of Projection A to the assertion of the creator in Projection C So-And-So remains a further projection that cannot be, a projection that is never projected into reality.

> The arrangement contains the desire of
> The artist. But one confides in what has no
> Concealed creator. One walks easily

>The unpainted shore, accepts the world
>As anything but sculpture. Good-bye,
>Mrs. Pappadopoulos, and thanks.

Through the series of projections and hypothetical ways of seeing a work of art, Stevens arrives once again at the rejection of the intentional structure. The intentional posing, the deliberate arrangement, at the same time alienate the artist from his creation and imprison him in it. In "So-And-So Reclining on Her Couch" Stevens comes back to the unpainted shore, the unordered world. In rejecting metaphor he accepts the gratuitousness of experience, accepts the world "as anything but sculpture." The last words, "Good-bye, Mrs. Pappadopoulos, and thanks," act out this rejection of intentional constructs by suggesting that the poem itself was a series of possible projections, a series of musings on an art-object and thus, like "The Man with the Blue Guitar," a series of diversions from reality.

The problem of artistic creation is thus not solved by the structure within the structure. The ballad and the porcelain of "Three Travelers Watch a Sunrise" and the sculpture of "So-And-So Reclining on Her Couch" are imagined structures in a world that the imagination has not humanized, has not rendered "habitable." "The statue is the sculptor, not the stone" (*OP*, 64). For Stevens the sculpture bears the mark of the artist, and it rejects and is rejected by reality: "But could the statue stand in Africa? / The marble was imagined in the cold" (*OP*, 56). The marble consciously created opposes itself to the unimaginable world. And to the enclosed space and the intentional creation is added a sense of coldness, a physical experience of desolation. But it is a physical experience that tends to deny all physical experience. The coldness of the imagined structure is the deathlike coldness of the art-object, raised out of the temporal, like Keats's "cold pastoral," and out of the realm of experience.

In rejecting metaphor Stevens begins to seek an experience that cannot be imagined, a simplicity beyond all the "intricate evasions" of structure. "Thought is false happiness," he begins in "Crude Foyer." It is false to think "that there lies at the end of

thought / A foyer of the spirit in a landscape / Of the mind." For
even though the foyer is to be found "at the end of thought," it is
still placed "in a landscape of the mind." The poet will have to
find a foyer not only "at the end of thought" but also "at the end
of the mind," one which will deny the validity of mental constructs. "The mind / Is the eye, and . . . this landscape of the
mind / Is a landscape only of the eye." The inner eye is caught in
the landscape it has created. But as in Wordsworth's poetry, the
inner vision does not coincide with the outer world. Elsewhere
Stevens argues that "the mind is smaller than the eye" (*CP*,
161). "We live in a place / That is not our own and, much more,
not ourselves" (*CP*, 383), and every attempt to make the world
"home" ends in deeper alienation:

> We are ignorant men incapable
> Of the least, minor, vital metaphor, content,
> At last, there, when it turns out to be here.

The metaphor is not "vital" but "vitally deprived." It is always a
"there," for it creates a temporal and spatial distance between the
poet and the object. The alien place may become "our own" and
the crude foyer a hearth of being only if the "thereness" of the
mental landscape gives way to the presence of reality.

The arrival at the "hereness" of reality remains essentially unexplained, particularly since Stevens is still dealing with the
possible revelation of language, a revelation which does not take
place. Even as he rejects the paper rose, he believes that "the
innermost good of their [the philosophers'] seeking / Might come
in the simplest of speech" (*CP*, 27), "as if the language suddenly,
with ease, / Said things it had laboriously spoken" (*CP*, 387).
The quest for simplicity begins with the word. To say what is unspeakable, the word must reach the essence of the object it names.
But the "simplest of speech" is a movement toward silence: "Is
there a poem that never reaches words?" (*CP*, 396). Stevens
speaks of "immaculate syllables" (*CP*, 188), an "immaculate
imagery" (*CP*, 250), suggesting that there is a point at which

the word and the object meet. But he cannot utter the syllable or create the imagery that might "secrete us in reality" (*CP*, 310).

Sight, like speech, is an impediment to poetic vision. "You must become an ignorant man again / And see the sun again with an ignorant eye" (*CP*, 380). But "something of the trouble of the mind / Remains in the sight" (*OP*, 97). The eye in Stevens *creates* a landscape of the mind and shares the mind's inability to penetrate the natural world. There is always a film of consciousness that turns reality into a mental landscape. For a moment, Stevens closes his eyes, refusing to see a reality that has been mediated by his conscious perception: "nothing has been lost, / Sight least, but metaphysical blindness gained, / The blindness in which seeing would be false" (*OP*, 94–95). The metaphysical blindness is a refusal to accept a mediated reality, a perception that is not "immaculate." But there can be no unmediated perception, as there can be no "immaculate" speech. "The sun / Must bear no name, gold flourisher, but be / In the difficulty of what it is to be" (*CP*, 381). "Things as they are" are changed not only by the poet's imaginative perception of them but by any verbal utterance that hinges on their reality. "Phoebus is dead, ephebe. But Phoebus was / A name for something that never could be named" (*CP*, 381). The poet's voice names only the absence of things, and his remembrance of their presence is a further testimony of his loss. His quest is thus for a word that is uttered and not uttered, for a voice that is speechless in its speech: "A sunken voice, both of remembering / And of forgetfulness, in alternate strain" (*CP*, 29). The forgetfulness of self would be a remembrance of reality, but a reality in which the creating self would be forgotten. The sunken voice would be unable to create, unable to pluck the strings of the blue guitar. Only a dual act of remembrance and forgetfulness, of assertion and denial of the conscious self "in alternate strain," could make the creative act suffice. But Stevens finds, like Rousseau, that artistic creation asserts the creative consciousness by opposing it to the natural world it tries to reach. There is always a reaching out toward reality, but never an experience, never a fulfillment: "A color that moved us with

forgetfulness. / When was it that we heard the voice of union?"
(*CP,* 494). Again in this passage forgetfulness is a means of
integration to reality. But the voice of union is also a voice of
silence, a "sunken voice" that suggests the dissolution of the self
in the natural world.

The Transformation of Consciousness

Whether withdrawing into the enclosed space of the intentional creation or dissolving into the natural world, the poet
stands blind and speechless in front of a reality he cannot reach or
re-create. The attempted re-creation of nature has proved for
Stevens, as for Yeats, a distancing from reality and a withdrawal
into a zone of consciousness where no creative act can suffice. But
Stevens begins much earlier than Yeats to redescend into reality,
seeking the object and the place in their moment of revelation.
The fleeting experience of such moments, rather than their description, can lead the poet to the place of being. Only if he seeks
to experience rather than capture, to perceive immaculately what
he cannot consciously re-create, can the alien place become
"home." From Wordsworth to Stevens the poetic act has ceased
its quest for totality in order to grasp reality as a series of experiences. Wordsworth is ultimately frightened by the unfathered
quality of the vapor and seeks to subsume its gratuitousness in the
workings of one great power. In general, however, gratuitousness
marks every valid experience in modern poetry. Suddenly and
without warning the object reveals its presence, and the poet
perceives unmediatedly what his poetry could not fathom. Thus
poetry begins to speak of its incapacity to reach the place of being,
or to create even a threshold where the significant experience may
take place. If it does take place, the experience seems more a
revelation than a deliberate creation. The poetic act reaches out,
but it cannot reach. It speaks of an experience, but the experience
is almost always virtual. Between silence and speech, poetry enacts
the tragedy of the conscious self.

Perhaps this core of silence in the poem, this sense of something virtual and imminent about to be realised, constitutes the threshold itself of the experience. The creative act ceases trying to name reality and begins instead to suggest its incapacity to reach a reality that is assuredly there. In turning against itself and denying the validity of the act that brings it into being, the poem revalidates the natural world. The effort and the failure are part of the same striving toward the unmediated experience of reality. To speak of a reality that cannot be reached through the poem is to assert the existence of a valid reality outside the poem and to make possible its gratuitous "divination."

The quest for the unmediated experience is marked by a passage from the abstract to the concrete, from the ascension into totality to "a letting down / From loftiness" (*OP,* 101), from the total grasping of reality to a more limited experience of a particular object in a particular place. In "Woman Looking at a Vase of Flowers," for instance, the formless and invisible forces become "realized" into distinguishable shapes. Shelley's west wind actualizes itself through the visible effects of its presence. In Stevens' poem the wind dissolves into birds, the clouds become braided girls, and the sea turns once more into wind seeking to destroy the frame that separates the poet from reality. As in "Domination of Black," the poet creates in the enclosed room. But the wind of reality in this poem seeks to penetrate the intentional world, destroying the "large abstraction" of artistic creation. Echoing the movement from the thunder to the piano and from the wind to the birds, in the second stanza the "high blue" of the sky becomes particularized in leaf and bud, so that the "looking at" of the title becomes a "looking into," a Wordsworthian seeing into the life of things. In a similar movement the red descends from its large abstraction and becomes slowly ingrained in specific objects in reality, "first, summer, then a lesser time, / Then the sides of peaches, of dusky pears." The large abstraction would seek a total grasping of reality. Only through this descent from the conceptual to the sides of peaches and dusky pears can the poem point to an immediate experience.

The descent into the particular is accompanied by a reduction

of time units, from the intemporal to the seasonal, then to a
"lesser time" that might lead to the moment of experience. The
abstractive imagination, which sought to humanize reality, has
found that abstraction and conceptualization are alienating
processes. The humanization of reality must on the contrary be
sought by a movement downward, as in Hölderlin's "Heimkunft,"
and by a progressive reduction of temporal and spatial distances
into the place and the moment of experience. In the third stanza
the inhuman colors become ingrained in reality, and as they do
they turn into "human conciliations," means of reattachment to
the real. The contact with reality is a momentary experience, a
sudden seeing into the object. Though Stevens seeks "the book of
reconciliation," the totality of the imagined book has here been
reduced to the suddenness and immediacy of an act—"a profounder reconciling, an act." Objects must be experienced "without clairvoyance," grasped immediately in their "thingness."

A similar reduction, this time in temporal distance, occurs in
"Of Bright & Blue Birds & the Gala Sun." In "Woman Looking
at a Vase of Flowers" the "high blue" of the sky passes into leaf
and bud. In "Of Bright & Blue Birds" the poet starts by looking
at particular objects and stresses the limited instant of reality.
Some things "instantly and in themselves" are gay. There is a
moment of fullness, an instant in which the self is complete in
itself. "And you and I are such things, O most miserable. . . ."
The misery stems from the irreparable opposition of consciousness
and reality. The child is complete by being unaware of his completeness, and the poet's awareness precludes any continuous sense
of completion. The fullness thus pertains to objects in reality,
bright and blue birds and the sun. But "for a moment" the poet
participates in their completeness. For a moment he comes out of
himself and becomes one with reality in a movement of joy.

The "they" of the second stanza, however, underlines once
more the distance between the poet and reality. Things are gay
"in themselves," and no outer or inner movement is required. But
the poet must move out of himself, out of the realm of the conscious self, in order to achieve joy. Ignorance and imperfection,

the rest of the poem suggests, are ultimately the valid means of
integration to reality, because they become transmuted into "a
gaiety that is being, not merely knowing." Yeats wanted to become "ignorant and wanton as the dawn"[15] in order to become
one with reality. Ignorance is for Stevens as well a mark of attachment to the natural world: "It may be that the ignorant
man, alone, / Has any chance to mate his life with life" (*CP*,
222). Ignorance is an "agreement" of the self with itself and with
the natural world. Through such agreement the self denies itself
possession of reality in order to participate in the plenitude of
things. To be both reality and consciousness of reality, "in that
element" and "in a way apart," the poet must think "without the
labor of thought," see beyond the consciousness of sight, reject
conceptual knowledge for an immediate cognition of the object.
The quest for totality has transmuted itself into a quest for the
particular. "The imperfect is our paradise" (*CP*, 194), and the
limited experience rather than the attempt to comprehend and
encompass reality becomes the valid quest for poetry, seeking as
Yeats suggests "knowledge lost in trance / Of sweeter ignorance."[16]
Stevens speaks of a body "swollen / With thought, through which
it cannot see" (*CP*, 354). "To think is to think the way to death"
(*CP*, 256), "as if to know became / The fatality of seeing things
too well" (*CP*, 459). Knowledge becomes the fatality of conscious
perception, an act of sight that denies the sudden insight into the
object.

This dialectic of permanence and immediacy, conceptual
thought and natural process, is explored further in "Sunday
Morning":

> Complacencies of the peignoir, and late
> Coffee and oranges in a sunny chair,
> And the green freedom of a cockatoo
> Upon a rug mingle to dissipate
> The holy hush of ancient sacrifice.

15. "The Dawn."
16. "Shepherd and Goatherd."

Coffee, oranges, sunny, green freedom, cockatoo—the first three lines of the poem bespeak a world of richness and abandonment, a slow merging into reality. But the ancient sacrifice encroaches upon the possible richness of Sunday morning, and as it does the "green freedom" of the opening lines passes into the darkening world of myth. The "encroachment of that old catastrophe" is the symbolic recurrence of the ancient sacrifice. But it is also the encroachment of consciousness upon a world with which consciousness cannot coexist. The transcendent and the conceptual, as in Wordsworth's "Intimations Ode," deny the immediate aspects of reality. "The pungent oranges and bright, green wings / Seem things in some procession of the dead" because the protagonist fails to grasp and experience these objects in their immediate and momentary reality and seeks instead the changeless, transcendent reality of myth. Religious myth becomes a deadening of reality, an "old catastrophe" periodically renewed.

This deadening movement is marked by the silence that falls upon everything touched by ancient myth—"hush, stilled, silent, without sound." Just as the "old catastrophe" darkens natural reality, the ceremony that repeats or re-enacts it silences the natural world. The world of myth is a world of devoid of sensory perception, where blindness and deafness reinforce the quest for the transcendent. Against this world the poet formulates a series of questions:

> Why should she give her bounty to the dead?
> What is divinity if it can come
> Only in silent shadows and in dreams?
> Shall she not find in comforts of the sun,
> In pungent fruit and bright, green wings, or else
> In any balm or beauty of the earth,
> Things to be cherished like the thought of heaven?
> Divinity must live within herself.

Rejecting the silent shadows which suggest the blindness and deafness that accompany the religious denial of sensory perception, Stevens asserts in interrogative form the capacity to find joy in objects in reality, objects not trapped in a procession toward the transcendent. These objects are caught instead in a world of process—"the bough of summer and the winter branch"—suggesting that there is a "divinity" in reality, a self-contained "sacrality" of things. Such a universe is divine precisely because it is godless. An abstract god dwelling in heaven desacralizes natural reality by making a withdrawal from the universe and an ascension into the invisible the prerequisites for human fulfillment. It is this kind of ascension that blinds Wordsworth to the natural world. Stevens in "Sunday Morning" rejects the drive toward transcendence and reasserts the validity of the here and now. The passage from immanence to transcendence is a "spiritous passage into nothingness" (*CP*, 56), a denial of reality when there is nothing else to assert. In order for the natural world to regain its "sacrality," heaven must be considered a tomb, and the sky must become part of the earth, not part of heaven:

> And shall the earth
> Seem all of paradise that we shall know?
> The sky will be much friendlier then than now,
> A part of labor and a part of pain,
> And next in glory to enduring love,
> Not this dividing and indifferent blue.

Only as the "colossal illusion of heaven" (*CP*, 241) is revealed does the sky rejoin the earth. The transcendent is then denied, the abstraction is "broken," conceptual thought is "blown away."

The rejection of heaven is usually given not as an assertion but as an improbable possibility: "If thinking could be blown away / Yet this remain the dwelling-place / Of those with a sense for simple space" (*CP*, 153). Even in the conditional tense the blowing away of thought remains the prerequisite for truly inhabiting the earth. And inhabiting the earth means discovering a particular, delimited space, a "simple space" as Stevens calls it, where man can both possess and participate in reality, retain his individual consciousness yet be at one with the natural world.

This stress on the particular, delimited place is given in "Extracts from Addresses to the Academy of Fine Ideas" as a passage from the "an" to the "the." The indefinite article impedes the discovery of the particular place of being. But if the self can delimit the infinite distances and turn them into "simple space," it can make of the empty place the foundation of being. The delimitation of space is seen as a way of reasserting the "being" of the conscious self in all the particularity of its existence. In a movement similar to that of "Sunday Morning," Stevens turns away once again from the abstraction. Shelley found that as he ascended Mont Blanc he reached the icy wasteland of the conceptual, and all descent was cut off by the self-destructive power of the imagination. Stevens moves from the "icy Elysée" of abstraction out and down into reality. Where Shelley is trapped by ice, in this poem the ice melts, water breaks into reality, and the elemental continuity of ice and water, broken not as in Shelley by the fire of the poetic imagination but by the seasonal forces, re-establishes contact with the natural world.

In "Landscape with Boat" Stevens returns to the themes of the false abstraction and the false heaven. The protagonist wants to arrive at the absolute truth, the unaltered image. But the passage toward the absolute is a passage into nothingness, for he must reach it

> by rejecting what he saw
> And denying what he heard. He would arrive.
> He had only not to live, to walk in the dark,
> To be projected by one void into
> Another.

The passage into the absolute-nothingness involves a denial of sensory perception and a rejection of anything touched by reality: "He wanted imperceptible air." To see the imperceptible and to hear the inaudible may be ways of arriving at the "unmediated vision." But the quest for the absolute truth blinds the perceiving eye and silences the poet on the threshold of what he thought might be the ultimate revelation. Instead of seeking the truth, Stevens begins to see multiple truths in a universe where diversity has taken precedence over the desire for a coherent structure. Just as the *the* is a way of experiencing the "thingness" of the

object, only the indefinite article *a* can take away from the truth
its destructive totality:

> It was when I said,
> "There is no such thing as the truth,"
> That the grapes seemed fatter.
> The fox ran out of his hole.   [*CP,* 203]

The turn from the absolute to the particular is what Stevens calls
"on the road home." "If nothing was the truth, then all / Things
were the truth, the world itself was the truth" (*CP,* 242). From
this Stevens moves to the position that even appearance, even
the false blue of the sky, may be part of the truth, for "in such
seeming all things are" (*CP,* 339). The perceiving eye changes
reality and is changed by it, no longer seeking the "imageless
truth" but an interchange between self and world.

In "Contrary Theses (II)" the abstract appears as the invisible
center which may or may not be there ("The abstract was suddenly there and gone again"), but the contours, the real things,
remain: "The flies / And the bees still sought the chrysanthe-
mums' odor." In rejecting the abstract aspect of truth the poet
finds himself returning to the long lost "simple-space":

> and we are content,
> In a world that shrinks to an immediate whole,
>
> That we do not need to understand, complete
> Without secret arrangements of it in the mind.
> ["Description without Place"]

There is a definite relationship between immediacy and wholeness
in this passage. As the world shrinks and infinite space is delimited into a recognizable place, the self finds itself "home," or
at least on the road home, "complete in a completed scene" (*CP,*
378). Completion suggests for Stevens a delimitation of reality in
which wholeness and totality are diametrically opposed.

The rejection of transcendence and the return to the particularity of the "the" also call for an acceptance of the momentary
experience, validated in and for itself. In "Waving Adieu, Adieu,

Adieu" Stevens affirms the infinite value of the moment that
passes and the thing that dies:

> In a world without heaven to follow, the stops
> Would be endings, more poignant than partings, profounder,
> And that would be saying farewell, repeating farewell,
> Just to be there and just to behold.

It is this instantaneous quality of every experience that the protagonist in "Sunday Morning" cannot accept:

> She says, "I am content when wakened birds,
> Before they fly, test the reality
> Of misty fields, by their sweet questionings;
> But when the birds are gone, and their warm fields
> Return no more, where, then, is paradise?"

The instant of experience is invalidated by her consciousness of
its temporality. Paradise, for the protagonist, would be the
changeless, eternal landscape, the total arrest of movement. "She
says, 'But in contentment I still feel / The need of some imperishable bliss.' " In opposition to this quest for changelessness and
immobility Stevens contends that permanence is to be found in
the world of process. April's green endures because it is caught in
the seasonal process. It endures, like Wordsworth's experiences
perhaps, because memory redeems it from its temporal finiteness.
But it endures, above all, *because* of its finiteness: "Death is the
mother of beauty." The experience is destroyed by time, but it
has been eternal in its instant, and in its temporal finiteness and
its death lies its endurance.

To his rejection of the abstract, the conceptual, the transcendent, Stevens adds the rejection of the changeless, deathless
landscape:

> Is there no change of death in paradise?
> Does ripe fruit never fall? Or do the boughs
> Hang always heavy in that perfect sky,
> Unchanging, yet so like our perishing earth,
> With rivers like our own that seek for seas
> They never find, the same receding shores
> That never touch with inarticulate pang?

Seasonal process is arrested in this paradise which the protagonist would term "imperishable bliss." There is a definite imminence of movement—boughs hanging, shores never touching—but it is an imminence which the changeless landscape turns into immobility. Like the figures on Keats's urn, forever about to accomplish an act that never takes place, the natural world in this stanza is taken out of its temporal context and is in this sense denaturalized. The raising of nature out of the temporal and into the eternal para- doxically turns deathlessness into a deadening of movement. Nature turns, precisely, into a mental landscape, a conceptual configuration that has kept little of reality. Instead of a world of imperishable bliss, there is "a world of universal poverty":

> In a world of universal poverty
> The philosophers alone will be fat
> Against the autumn winds
> In an autumn that will be perpetual.
>   ["Like Decorations in a Nigger Cemetery"]

The autumn winds may be agents of change, but the philosophers construct a perpetual autumn where no winds, no movement, no process may take place—a landscape of the mind that usurps the reality of the natural world and unrealizes the self: "to be real each had / To find for himself his earth, his sky, his sea" (*CP*, 312).

This stress on the limited experience is further explored in "Credences of Summer." Seasonal time is central to the poem. In the first section of the poem summer is an overwhelming season: "the roses are heavy with a weight / Of fragrance and the mind lays by its trouble." Even though the first stanza speaks of spring and autumn, summer seems to overcome the seasonal process, denying, by its very completeness, any before or after. Like Eliot's "midwinter spring" in "Little Gidding," midsummer suggests for Stevens the height of fulfillment, "beyond which there is nothing left of time." Even memory, which almost inevitably introduces a consciousness of temporality, is here reduced to "fidgets of remembrance." The consciousness of time is destroyed in the fullness of the season, and this temporal stasis creates a certain space in summer, a landscape of pine and sun: "The day / Enriches the year . . . / Stripped of remembrance, it displays its strength." Remembrance, in fact, opposes itself to temporal fulfillment. Devoid of memory, the day is also freed of the movement from before to after. It reveals itself in all its fullness, impelled by a life of its own, without exterior cause. "One man becomes a race, / Lofty like him, like him perpetual." The eternal is born out of the temporally limited experience. The moment, the season, the object become the "axis of everything," the center of the world.

Stevens avoids in this poem an analysis of the experience. In "The Man with the Blue Guitar" he had suggested at the end that there would be moments in which the poet, consciously departing from reality, would "choose to play / The imagined pine, the imagined jay." In "Credences of Summer" he deliberately postpones "the anatomy of summer, as / The physical pine, the metaphysical pine." Poetry ceases being a metaphysical game and becomes an instrument to experience the real, a mental construct that must somehow reach the physical reality of things:

> Let's see the very thing and nothing else.
> Let's see it with the hottest fire of sight.
> Burn everything not part of it to ash.

Stevens again limits the scope of his vision to the particular object and the specific place of the experience. He seeks to penetrate the object in its temporal aspects and in so doing reach its moment of "presence," a moment that reveals the "essential barrenness" of the object, "right ignorance / Of change still possible." Though seasonal changes will take place, for a moment the object is the "centre" of time and therefore timeless. "The barrenness that appears is an exposing. / It is not part of what is absent" (*CP*, 487). Barrenness, in fact, becomes synonymous with presence: "This is the barrenness / Of the fertile thing that can attain no more." Fertility reveals something essential and eternal by asserting rather than denying the barrenness it apparently opposes.

Between the discovery of barrenness and the recognition of

fertility, there is a virtual experience in a poem that wishes to become "pure rhetoric of a language without words." But the problem with most of Stevens' longer poems is that they theorize about themselves without providing an enactment of their project. The "there" becomes a "here" through an affirmation that the poem does not prepare and cannot sustain. The shorter poems are more successful because they can more easily turn against themselves and become willful decreations. The self cannot live in a world that has not been in some measure humanized by the imagination. But neither can it live in a world constructed entirely "in nature's spite." The "description without place" abstracts and conceptualizes the experience, it annihilates the present and is left at the end with "an absence in reality." To return to the reality from which it has "issued," the imagination must turn in upon itself and become the pathway to a place without description. Only the return to the instant in which reality becomes present—beyond all seeming—and the deliberate undercutting of the poem's capacity to transform that reality can lead to the moment and the place of being. "In the instant of speech, / The breadth of an accelerando moves, / Captives the being, widens— and was there" (*CP,* 440). Within the pastness of the poetic structure there is a virtual presentness that the poem enfolds and may reveal. The acknowledgment of the poem as a "was" bespeaks a movement toward that virtual, unspoken "is." By understanding its limitations, consciousness begins to transform itself.

The first step toward this transformation of consciousness, as Stevens has been suggesting intermittently since *Parts of a World,* is the affirmation of a reality outside the realm of the imagination, a reality that remains untouched and unapproachable. In "Autumn Refrain" the poet seeks out a world he cannot name and which is given only as an evasion: "the moon and moon, / The yellow moon of words. . . ." The naming of the objects creates an absence, a disjunction between the concept and the thing, the moon and moon. The nightingale is the "name" of the thing never to be seen or heard. The name and the air are "evasions of the nightingale," linguistic structures that the objects elude. Yet there remains, beneath the objects named, an undefinable reality, "some skreaking and skrittering residuum" that points to the nightingale and the song precisely as evasions.

Still more pointedly in "Not Ideas about the Thing but the Thing Itself," an outside reality which the poet finds hard to define seems to intrude and force its way into the poem. A cry that the poet hears seems at first to be lodged in his mind: "a scrawny cry from outside / Seemed like a sound in his mind." In the enclosed space of the imagination, all reality tends to originate in the mind. Yet the bird's cry, and the sun, point with increasing insistence to an exterior reality: "The sun was coming from outside. . . . It was like / A new knowledge of reality." The outside world has swept into the walled-in consciousness, forcing the poet to recognize a reality that has eluded the imagination, a reality that is a *new* knowledge, not fully apprehended.

This intrusion of natural reality into the poet's inner world is accompanied by an "awakening" of the poet to a reality he had forgotten:

> I wonder, have I lived a skeleton's life,
> As a questioner about reality,
>
> A countryman of all the bones of the world?
> Now, here, the warmth I had forgotten becomes
>
> Part of a major reality, part of
> An appreciation of reality.   ["First Warmth"]

In the enclosed room of the imagination (the other version of the poem is titled "As You Leave the Room"), the poet begins to question his questioning of reality. The outside world has forced its way into his consciousness and in doing so it has forced the poet into an awareness of the skeletal quality of his imaginative world.[17]

17. As J. Hillis Miller points out in *Poets of Reality: Six Twentieth-Century Writers* (Cambridge: Harvard University Press, 1966), p. 242, Stevens is suggesting that these things he enumerates in "As You Leave the Room" are not things a skeleton thinks about. In this version, what the poet has forgotten is not "warmth" but "snow" ("Now, here, the snow I had forgotten . . ."). Be it snow or warmth, reality returns to his

A similar stress on an exterior, unimagined reality occurs in "Bouquet of Roses in Sunlight" and "The Green Plant." Things as they are are no longer changed by the blue guitar in these poems. Instead, Stevens speaks of the inability of the metaphor to "image" reality:

> Too much as they are to be changed by metaphor,
> Too actual, things that in being real
> Make any imaginings of them lesser things.
>   ["Bouquet of Roses in Sunlight"]

In speaking of the primacy of an exterior reality, the poem suggests at the same time its inability to validly reconstruct the natural world. The metaphoric arrangement of the flowers leaves them no longer "as they are." But the imagination is fully aware of its capacity for betrayal:

> How clean the sun when seen in its idea,
> Washed in the remotest cleanliness of a heaven
> That has expelled us and our images . . .
>   ["Notes Toward a Supreme Fiction"]

For the sun to retrieve its reality the poetic images had to be expelled, broken through—which means their limitations recognized. The snowman may have been a cold nothingness because he lacked the capacity to imagine, but the imaginative man must make himself "the blank mechanic of the mountains, / The blank frere of fields" (*CP,* 492) in order not to create an absence in reality. In this respect, the absence is carried from reality into the imagination. Through the consciousness of its insufficiency the imagination creates its own vacancy, and the ontological primacy passes once more into reality: "The world images for the beholder" (*CP,* 492). It is no longer the imagination that consciously reconstructs the natural world but the world that arranges itself into patterns to be perceived by the imagination. The imaginative act is here infused with the sense of process pertaining to the natural world, as if the natural world had acquired a

---

imaginative world. See also Bloom, *The Ringers,* p. 281: "Stevens, in the final finding of the ear, returned to the snow he had forgotten, to behold again 'nothing that is not there and the nothing that is.' "

certain ordering intelligence, as if reality itself had brought into being the imaginative act that might destroy it. The beholder no longer possesses his act of perception, he is instead possessed by the object of perception—"the possessed of sense not the possessor" (*CP,* 492). When the sense "lies still" the poet is engulfed by a reality he could not otherwise reach: "So sense exceeds all metaphor." And again: "It is to disclose the essential presence, say, / Of a mountain, expanded and elevated almost / Into a sense" (*CP,* 531). The deliberate undercutting of image and metaphor in Stevens' poetry gives back to sensory perception its revelatory value. Instead of the poem taking the place of a mountain word for word, the mountain here is not verbally reconstructed. It is "felt" as an object whose immediacy has suddenly irrupted into the poetic consciousness.

There is a similar irruption of the object on the poetic consciousness in "The Green Plant." Summer passes into autumn, and this passage is given as a movement into artificiality: the lion roses have turned to paper roses, and the autumn colors appear as dimmed and falsified reflections of the sun. The organic process has given way to mechanical images: paper, wrecked umbrellas, shadows of trees. There is a sense of unreality in the poem even before reality has been brought into question. Even the forest is a painted forest ("the maroon and olive forest"), a legendary place.

But the green plant suggests a permanence of the natural process, a persistence of reality in spite of the shadows and the dimming sun. In the midst of autumn, it "glares, outside of the legend, with the barbarous green / Of the harsh reality of which it is part." It rejects the stylization of the shadow, the reflection, the word on paper, and refuses to be "managed and mastered" (*OP,* 238), thus asserting the existence of a reality outside the realm of the imagination. The imaginative act, in Stevens' poetry, brings forth "a constant secondariness." But this recognition of its limitation makes it point beyond itself, to a place at the end of the mind. The landscape of the poem seems to want to force the green plant into the "finality" of its dimness. But the barbarous green remains, precisely, a barbarous green, unmediated or toned

down by the conscious creation. The poem that speaks of a
natural object eluding the legend speaks at the same time of its
own incapacity to grasp the object in its barbarous reality. "Silence
is a shape that has passed," but silence seems to be always at the
center of Stevens' later poems.

Silence, of course, is part of Stevens' quest for the present—
and presence. "The poet speaks the poem as it is, / Not as it was"
(*CP*, 473). But speech constantly throws him back into the
pattern of temporality, forcing upon him Lenin's vision of past
and future and a joyless description without place:

> The swans fled outward to remoter reaches,
> As if they knew of distant beaches; and were
>
> Dissolved. The distances of space and time
> Were one and swans far off were swans to come.
>
> The eye of Lenin kept the far-off shapes.
> His mind raised up, down-drowned, the chariots.
>
> And reaches, beaches, tomorrow's regions became
> One thinking of apocalyptic legions.

Lenin's vision conceives the swans far-off, in the distances of past
and future, unifying memory and projection by denying the
presence of the real. Temporal continuity entails a disjunction
between perception and vision: without swans to perceive, the
apocalyptic vision seems to extend the already vast distances, dissolving the poet's focus on reality.

A similar treatment of the subject, but with a different resolution, occurs in "Wild Ducks, People and Distances":

> There remained the smoke of the villages. Their fire
> Was central in distances the wild ducks could
> Not span, without any weather at all, except
> The weather of other lives, from which there could
>
> Be no migrating. It was that they were there
> That held the distances off: the villages
> Held off the final, fatal distances,
> Between us and the place in which we stood.

The poet begins here on the outside, in the vast distances of earth

and sky, and moves, in opposition to Lenin's vision in "Description without Place," toward a more definite, more particular
perception of reality. Lenin tries to encompass time and space and
is to some extent engulfed by his vision. In "Wild Ducks, People
and Distances" the dissolution of perception into vision is held off
by the smoke, the wild ducks, and the villages—the landmarks of
the poet's reality. One landmark in reality holds off the dissolution of another, and the world is held together by a series of
perceptions and recognitions. There was nothing in "Description
without Place" to keep the swans from flying into temporal space.
But though the wild ducks in this poem will migrate to other
climates, the fire and smoke of the villages create a place in reality
"from which there could / Be no migrating."

The distances are thus held off because the landmarks hold the
place together. It is as if distance, by these specific landmarks,
were kept from becoming "distant," as if space were commanded
to be a "simple space" rather than a "category of dispossession."[18]
The sense of "simple space" ultimately holds off the fatal distances
and the protagonist's dissolution into infinite space, and affirms
the place in which the poet stands as the simple space of being.
There is to be no migrating for the protagonist, but then no
migrating is possible where distance does not exist. Denying the
existence of anything valid outside their rigidly structured space,
the villages deny the fatal distances between the poet and the
immediate reality of his world.

Once more the poet has rejected the infinite distances, visionary
unity, and temporal continuity, for the simple space and the
present instant of experience:

> It is better for me
> In the rushes of autumn wind
> To embrace autumn, without turning
> To remember summer.
>
> . . . . .
> The man of autumn,
> Behind its melancholy mask,

---

18. Bonnefoy, *L'Improbable* (Paris: Mercure de France, 1959), p. 149.

> Will laugh in the brown grass,
> Will shout from the tower's rim.   ["Secret Man"]

Almost with the resonance of Yeats's "Those Images," Stevens' secret man refuses to remember, refuses to be cast in temporal duration. He chooses rather to move with the seasons, and this immersion in the natural process brings forth, as in "Of Bright & Blue Birds & the Gala Sun," "a laughter, an agreement, by surprise." Memory and prophecy, the movements away from the present which made Lenin's swans fly off into remoter reaches, are rejected in order

> to feel again
> The reconciliation, the rapture of a time
> Without imagination, without past
> And without future, a present time.   ["Owl's Clover"]

Significantly, and disturbingly, the reconciliation occurs through a denial of the imagination, as if the imagination itself were the force compelling the poet to move into past and future, denying him the capacity for immediate experience. Wordsworth speaks of his childhood relationship to nature as a time of rapture, a time which is always now because it is lodged in the natural, not the temporal world. The temporal and the natural, in this passage from "Owl's Clover," appear disjointed by the conscious imagination. Reconciliation comes only as the imagination is denied, only as the consciousness of temporality gives way to a total commitment to the present. With increasing frequency Stevens begins to doubt, in his later poetry, the capacity of the imagination to bring forth the "profounder reconciling" of consciousness and reality.

Yet poetry cannot sustain a denial of the imagination that brings it into being. Though the time of rapture may be a time without imagination, though the secret man may refuse to remember summer in order to embrace autumn, the poetic imagination must find a way to transform consciousness without denying it, a way to reach the present without destroying the temporal duration in which it exists. Thus instead of seeking "the rapture of a time / Without imagination" Stevens begins to force the imagination to create a barren landscape which will ultimately reveal the fertile land: "Is there an imagination . . . which in the midst of summer stops / To imagine winter?" (*CP*, 417). The seasonal movement is here arrested, and the imagination introduces into the natural world a temporal projection of an absent season. The secret man refused to stop and remember, for memory and prophecy would undercut the moment of plenitude and transport him from the natural into the temporal world. But Stevens is suggesting in "The Auroras of Autumn" that the imagining of winter in the midst of summer creates a barrenness which enfolds an essential fertility, which is revelation rather than absence, a possible meeting of the temporal and the natural worlds. Barrenness becomes in the later poems the condition of a possible plenitude, and the end of the imagination points to a renewed presence of reality.

The imagination thus begins to create a barren landscape as the necessary stage for the poetic experience. Sometimes, as in "Vacancy in the Park," the barren stage is set but no experience is enacted:

> March . . . Someone has walked across the snow,
> Someone looking for he knows not what.

The poem opens in the past tense, speaking of an undefined "someone" who has walked and is no longer there. The footsteps in the snow are the visible traces of his passage, but their presence suggests an absence, they bear witness to an event that has passed. Their presence in fact introduces into the poem a dual sense of absence and pastness, and seems to dissolve the reality of what remains. The undefined someone seeking an undefined something turns the vacancy of the landscape into a doubt about the existence of reality. The protagonist marches through the park and through the season a little like the protagonist in Robbe-Grillet's *Dans le labyrinthe,* ignorant of his destination or the object of his search, saying only "Il fallait y aller, pour savoir" (it was necessary to go there in order to know). But there is no arrival in this vacancy in

the park. The footsteps point to something that was—the passage
of the protagonist—and this act of passage points in turn to something that has not been—the arrival at a significant something
which has not taken place. Pastness, absence, vacancy construct
an empty stage for the poetic act to take place.

But the following similes reinforce the sense of vacancy of the
first couplet:

> It is like a boat that has pulled away
> From a shore at night and disappeared.
>
> It is like a guitar left on a table
> By a woman, who has forgotten it.
>
> It is like the feeling of a man
> Come back to see a certain house.

In all three instances something is abandoned, or something is
lost. And the figure that has passed, the boat that has disappeared,
the guitar that is left, the man who returns to find that there is
no return, point to an absence that merges with a sense of pastness. The search in the vacancy of the park uncovers only a deeper
absence, a sense of infinite distance and emptiness that the protagonist cannot overcome. The only objects that the poem names,
and which landmark and give coherence to reality, dissolve and
disappear—the someone who in the time of the poem is not there,
the boat that has gone, and the silent guitar—so that at the end
there is only the wind to blow "in an empty place":

> The four winds blow through the rustic arbor,
> Under its mattresses of vines.

It is as if the essence of the poetic act in this poem were to sustain
the vacancy, turning it into a deepening absence, until only the
intangible winds remain.

A similar emptiness, and a profound doubt about the reality of
imaginative creation, inform the opening of "The Rock":

> The houses still stand,
> Though they are rigid in rigid emptiness.
>
> .   .   .   .   .

> The lives these lived in the mind are at an end.
> They never were . . . The sounds of the guitar
>
> Were not and are not.

The imagination has become the fictive covering of the rock, creating an illusion of order and fruitfulness in an otherwise infertile and alien reality.

> It is not enough to cover the rock with leaves.
> We must be cured of it by a cure of the ground
> Or a cure of ourselves, that is equal to a cure
>
> Of the ground, a cure beyond forgetfulness.

The leaves cover reality with a semblance of order. But they do not spring from reality, they do not "break into bud" from the arid rock. How can these intentional constructs validly "cure" a reality that is chaotic, barren, and alien? How can poetry be turned into a meaningful act?

> After the leaves have fallen, we return
> To a plain sense of things. It is as if
> We had come to an end of the imagination,
> Inanimate in an inert savoir.   ["The Plain Sense of Things"]

The falling of the leaves points to the imagination's recognition of the barrenness that underlies eveɪy attempt at creation, but it suggests at the same time the imagination's realization that in questioning its capacity to transform and reconstruct reality it is capable of perceiving reality in its "plainness" and its "thingness." This "inevitable knowledge" is ultimately "the cure / Of leaves and of the ground and of ourselves" (*CP*, 527). Abandoning its attempt to transform reality into meaning, the imagination begins to transform itself. It ceases to create a "landscape of the mind" (*CP*, 305) in order to reach "a land beyond the mind" (*CP*, 252). It rejects its own projections and diversions from reality and turns inward to reveal its incapacity to validly create and inhabit the world. There is no longer in "The Plain Sense of Things" a quest for "a time / Without imagination" but an acceptance of an imagination that has consciously turned against itself.

The Unmediated Experience

If consciousness and imagination are the alienating entities that separate the poet from the natural world, the imaginative act that undercuts its own validity brings the poem into contact with natural time, a time that is not time but season, a temporal "region" that partially unveils itself yet does not yield to us its secret or its significance. In "The Region November," for instance, the wind moves once more through a reality that has not been imaginatively articulated. All that can be said is that the treetops sway,

> Saying and saying, the way things say
> On the level of that which is not yet knowledge:
>
> A revelation not yet intended.

November is not a month but a region, a place in natural time, enclosing within itself the "saying" of the treetops. The imagination refuses to infuse, symbolically or metaphorically, this natural space with human meaning. Yet its refusal to transform and render meaningful a natural reality is itself an approach, an entrance into the month, the region. Like the wind that cannot utter the meaningful syllable, the imagination begins to speak on the mode of "saying" of the trees, approaching the objects without uncovering their meaning, swaying with the treetops in the wind without articulating syllables and conceptualizing a knowledge not yet attained. In refusing to "say," the imagination acquires in this poem the capacity to "say" of the wind and trees, pointing to a knowledge, a revelation, a discovery that cannot, rationally, take place. In Shelley's "Ode to the West Wind" the poetic imagination achieves a final fusion with the wind through a paradoxical affirmation of the poetic consciousness. In "The Region November" the imagination becomes one with the wind precisely through a denial of its capacity to become one with the natural world. The wind's incapacity to utter the meaningful syllable and the imagination's refusal to articulate it set both the wind and the poetic imagination "on the waste throne of [their] own wilderness," ruling over this temporal region as long as they guard its secret and bar the entrance to its world.[19]

The poet begins by hearing the wind and watching the tree-tops. But the objective observer is slowly woven into the temporal region, entering reality where meaning is not. It is as if the last couplet of the poem—"deeplier, deeplier, loudlier, loudlier, / The trees are swaying, swaying, swaying"—were an entrance into the poem and into reality by its evident inability to say anything *about* reality, anything beyond the swaying of the trees. In the imagination's discovery of its waste throne and its wilderness, the "saying" and the "swaying" for the first time become one. In becoming one with the wind, the imagination becomes the second blowing of the wind of "Valley Candle," the sudden draught that destroys image and metaphor and returns the candle to the night. In destroying itself, in deliberately creating its own wilderness, the poetic imagination enters the world it could not reach. "Always there is another life, / A life beyond this present knowing" (*OP,* 101). This is, perhaps, "the redeeming thought" (*CP,* 257). Rejecting the conceptual knowledge from which it springs in order to intuit the saying which is not yet knowledge, and denying its ability to enter a world from which consciousness is excluded, the imagination suddenly finds itself *in* reality, unable to articulate it but drawing the reader into the inexplicable experience.

In "Long and Sluggish Lines" Stevens takes up again the theme of the "saying" of the trees:

> The trees have a look as if they bore sad names
> And kept saying over and over one same, same thing.

Yet this statement—with its negative implications—is precisely the opposite of that of "The Region November." The trees in "Long and Sluggish Lines" say over and over the same thing *because* they look as if they bore sad names. They are contained

---

19. "The poem must resist the intelligence / Almost successfully" ("Man Carrying Thing," *CP,* 350).

in the rhetorical act. In "The Region November" the poet can only say that the trees sway, and he and they refuse to utter the words that might place the natural object within the infinite progression of rhetoric.

The end of "Long and Sluggish Lines," however, suggests a possible breakthrough of poetry from the rhetorical to the creative act:

> . . . Wanderer, this is the pre-history of February.
> The life of the poem in the mind has not yet begun.
>
> You were not born yet when the trees were crystal
> Nor are you now, in this wakefulness inside a sleep.

There is a strong suggestion here that the poem will bring forth the spring by breaking through the sleep of rhetoric.

To break through the sleep, of course, requires a deepening awareness of the limitations of the conscious act, the kind of awareness we find in "The Region November." What we get in Stevens' later poetry is a poetic consciousness simultaneously destroyed and transcended by consciousness itself. It is in this context that poetry is truly a destructive force (*CP*, 192). "The poem lashes more fiercely than the wind" (*CP*, 239), but its destructiveness is directed against consciousness, and against itself. Only through this process can the poetic imagination become a vehicle toward the unmediated experience. The "redeeming thought" is the recognition of its insufficiency; its rejection by the natural world is the way to a final reconciliation. Consciousness has been transformed by paradoxically moving to annihilate itself. And the poem has touched the unimaginable reality by undercutting the creative act that generated it. As creation and decreation become simultaneous, and in fact a single act, Stevens' poetry becomes the rite of passage into a world that lies beyond its reach.

It is perhaps "Of Mere Being," even more than "The Region November," that comes closest to the unmediated experience. Here the poem seems to stretch itself ineffably to the point of breakage in an attempt to "poematize" the mere being it cannot reach. Held off from the being at the end of the mind, yet painfully close, the poet re-creates the tension and desolation at the heart of the experience:

> The palm at the end of the mind,
> Beyond the last thought, rises
> In the bronze [decor],
>
> A gold-feathered bird
> Sings in the palm, without human meaning,
> Without human feeling, a foreign song.[20]

The object is placed at the end of the mind, beyond the last thought, in a realm that eludes imaginative penetration. Because the real eludes the imaginative, the imagination acquires a consciousness of intentionality which allows it to envision a reality beyond itself, though of course it is this very consciousness of intentionality which makes it posit an object at the end of the mind in the first place. We could see in this poem the same tautology and the same entrapment that we find in "The Man on the Dump."

In the first two lines the imagination strains toward the "real" object it has posited, and reality in turn "rises" on a world that had always rejected it. There is no sudden irruption of reality into the world of the imagination in this poem: the rising of the palm appears as a slow dawning, mirrored in the last stanza by the slow movement of the wind through the branches. But the first two lines suggest not so much the imagination's attempt to establish contact with reality as they do its attempt to break through its own enclosed space, its own infinite progression of images. The imagination posits a "real" world without attempting to "encounter" it. But paradoxically the object "rises" *in* imaginative space. The bronze decor underlines this imaginative perspective, the mental space within which reality is posited.

Yet this very opposition between "decor" and reality enacts in the poem the dialectical relationship of nature and imagination. The imagination's acknowledgment that the palm rises in a

20. "Decor" appears in *The Palm at the End of the Mind: Selected Poems and a Play,* ed. Holly Stevens (New York: Knopf, 1971). In *Opus Posthumous* the word is "distance."

bronze decor is an acknowledgment of dispossession, of its inability to reach, touch, or feel the immediacy of the natural world. The tension between decor and an object that rises "from" it but lies "beyond the last thought" suggests that the imagination recognizes its entrapment and its alienation. Paradoxically, this recognition generates in the poem an experience both of distance and proximity—of the remoteness of reality and of its imminent apparition. The imagination sees itself as an impediment between the poet and reality, yet that very insight allows it to go beyond the bronze decor, precisely into the land it claims is beyond its reach. The bronze decor is, paradoxically, an affirmation of imaginative enclosure and that which allows the imagination to move beyond its limits. It suggests dispossession as well as potential presence, and thus a world whose enclosure breaks down the moment it is stated. The imagination is *in* the bronze decor, yet posits a world beyond it. Decor suggests enclosure, but the imagination creates distance, and distance is a space that may be traversed. The sense of the remoteness of reality is precisely what allows the palm at the end of the mind to "rise" as an alien object in imaginative space. For the palm is "there," and in its "thereness" we are no longer "here." We are *in* the world, and it is *of* it. The presence of the object makes the imagination appear as an intruder, but intrusion is already the contact whose impossibility the poem proclaims.

A similar movement occurs in the second stanza. The bird's song suggests the impenetrable nature of reality. It is "without human meaning, / Without human feeling, a foreign song." Yet its very foreignness points to the unreality of the imaginative space of the poem. In positing an object alien to its space, the poem paradoxically "realizes" that object and undermines its own reality. It is the poetic imagination, in turn, that becomes foreign. It is the human who finds himself the alien in a world constructed in opposition to the natural. In positing a world beyond the enclosed space and terming it "foreign," the imagination undercuts its own space, its own enclosure, and moves out into the space it cannot reach. Remoteness becomes proximity. And the decor turns out to be "the edge of space." In hearing the foreign song of the bird the imagination does not try to humanize it but rather tends to silence itself in order to reach, as in "The Region November," the meaninglessness of the wind and the song and the silence of the trees. Turning against itself in order to experience reality, the imagination begins to silence itself on the threshold of being. The palm at the end of the mind and the song without human meaning create an absence in the poem, and the poem begins to drown in the plenitude it cannot encompass. The decor dissolves into the space it has both posited and negated, and the absence in the poem makes possible the dawning of reality. The poet in "Key West" could not draw meaning out of the "inhuman" but "veritable ocean" without reordering reality, and his rage for order thus went unassuaged. There is no rage for order in this poem. The poetic imagination is silencing itself before it can speak, placing reality in a realm into which it cannot transgress.

There is thus a core of silence in the poem, a refusal to image, order, or transform the natural world. The poetic imagination cannot inhabit reality. But it can experience reality by thrusting the poem into the silence of mere being. The recognition of its alienation from reality is precisely and paradoxically what overcomes that alienation. The poem that recognizes its intentionality, its imaginative enclosure, becomes a pathway into the realm of being. "Perception as an act of intelligence / And perception as an act of grace / Are two quite different things" (*OP*, 39). The poem, originating in the mind, destroys itself in the consciousness of its intentionality. And in that destruction it becomes, paradoxically, the poem in the act of finding—finding and experiencing a reality outside itself.

In *The Necessary Angel* Stevens tells us that "the great poems of heaven and hell have been written and the great poem of the earth remains to be written" (p. 142). To write this poem of the earth, poetry must transcend its own rhetoric and its posing of reality within imaginative constructs or progressions. It must, in fact, somehow get past the firecat of "Earthy Anecdote," without waiting for the firecat to fall asleep.

> Every time the bucks went clattering
> Over Oklahoma
> A firecat bristled in the way.
>
> Wherever they went,
> They went clattering,
> Until they swerved
> In a swift, circular line
> To the right,
> Because of the firecat.
>
> Or until they swerved
> In a swift, circular line
> To the left,
> Because of the firecat.
>
> The bucks clattered.
> The firecat went leaping,
> To the right, to the left,
> And
> Bristled in the way.
>
> Later, the firecat closed his bright eyes
> And slept.

The imagination first stands in the way of the poet's unmediated perception of reality and forces him to play a game with it, until the firecat falls asleep. It is perhaps fitting that in discussing the last poems of *Opus Posthumous* we return to the first of the *Collected Poems*. The need for such a return suggests that perhaps there has been not so much change in the poet's perspective as understanding of how such change may be brought about. Perhaps, indeed, Stevens' poetic career may be seen as a series of attempts to get past that firecat, arriving finally at the "method" which succeeds. "Earthy Anecdote" recognizes the problem of the rhetorical imagination. "The Region November" and "Of Mere Being" know how to transcend it.[21]

21. We find also in "The Planet on the Table" this desire to make the poem part of the earth:

> It was not important that they [the poems] survive.
> What mattered was that they should bear
> Some lineament or character,

From the enclosed space of "Domination of Black," the poetic imagination has moved outward into reality. It has denied the validity of its re-creation of the world in order to become a vehicle of experience. It has silenced itself on the threshold of reality so that reality could manifest itself. It has transformed the pastness of the poetic structure by creating an eternal present at the very heart of its temporality. Instead of fragmenting and re-ordering reality, possessing the "inert" secret of its creation, it has destroyed itself in the consciousness of its intentionality so that reality could become an experience both gratuitous and induced: "Not an attainment of the will / But something illogically received" (*OP*, 101), not a deliberate restructuring but a sudden revelation. Induced because the poetic imagination initiates the experience; gratuitous because in turning against itself it both poses and destroys its distance from reality and allows the entrance into the poem of an unimaginable world. Poetry has ceased being an instrument of domination to become a vehicle toward the experience of being. In limiting and undermining itself the poetic imagination has touched briefly the unimagined reality. It has brought us to the threshold of the "simple space" and silenced itself before it could fragment and reconstruct it. And in deliberately creating a void at the center of the poetic structure, the "absence for the poem" has finally turned, "at the end of the mind," into the presence of reality.

Some affluence, if only half-perceived,
In the poverty of their words,
Of the planet of which they were part.

This quest for the poetry of the earth once again takes us back to the "Earthy Anecdote" with which the *Collected Poems* begin.

꣓ INDEX

The Limits of Imagination

Designed by R. E. Rosenbaum.
Composed by York Composition Company, Inc.,
in 11 point Intertype Baskerville, 2 points leaded,
with display lines in Monotype Baskerville.
Printed letterpress from type by York Composition Company
on Warren's Number 66 text, 50 pound basis.
Bound by John H. Dekker & Sons, Inc.
in Joanna book cloth
and stamped in All Purpose foil.

Library of Congress Cataloging in Publication Data
(For library cataloging purposes only)

Regueiro, Helen, 1943-
    The limits of imagination.

    Includes bibliographical references and index.
    1. Wordsworth, William, 1770-1850—Criticism and interpretation. 2.
Yeats, William Butler, 1865-1939 — Criticism and interpretation. 3.
Stevens, Wallace, 1879-1955—Criticism and interpretation. 4. Imagina-
tion. I. Title.
PR5888.R4   821'.009   76-13663
ISBN 0-8014-0994-2